INTRODUCTION TO NOMAD™ REAL ESTATE INVESTING

THE REAL ESTATE INVESTING
MENTOR
THE AFFORDABLE $50K COACHING ALTERNATIVE

James Orr
The Real Estate Financial Planner™

Published by:

Real Estate Financial Planner LLC
PO Box 2163
Loveland CO 80539

https://RealEstateFinancialPlanner.com

First edition November 2024.
File: 2024-11-05 - Introduction to Nomad™ Real Estate Investing

This publication is designed to provide accurate and authoritative information regarding the subject matter covered. It is sold with the understanding that the publisher is not engaged in rendering legal, accounting or other professional advice or services. If legal advice or other expert advice is required, the services of a competent professional person should be sought.

From a *Declaration of Principles* jointly adopted by a Committee of American Bar Association and a Committee of Publishers and Associations.

This is a work of fiction. References to clients in this book are fictional and have been modified and changed from any possible real situations to protect the identities of clients and to simplify the stories for clarity. In some cases, significant parts of the stories have been changed. In some cases, stories have been completely fabricated to illustrate a concept. Any similarities to people alive or dead is purely coincidental.

AI Disclosure: While James Orr authored the original version of this content, AI was used extensively to draft, proofread, edit, improve and write subsequent versions and variations.

DEDICATION

Dedicated to my wife Tammy. I have no words.

FREE DOWNLOAD

The World's Greatest Real Estate Deal Analysis Spreadsheet™

Thank you for purchasing this book and taking the next step toward mastering real estate investing.

As a special bonus, you can download *The World's Greatest Real Estate Deal Analysis Spreadsheet*™ for free. This powerful tool will help you analyze deals like a pro, ensuring you make informed, profitable decisions.

Download your free copy now and start running the numbers with confidence.

https://REFP.com/spreadsheet

Table of Contents

Introduction to Nomad™ Real Estate Investing

The Nomad™ real estate investing strategy is a powerful way to acquire a portfolio or rental properties with little or no down payment and lower owner-occupant mortgage interest rates.

- **Minimal Upfront Investment** - Start your portfolio with as little as 0% down (USDA/VA loans), 3% (conventional), 3.5% (FHA), or typically 5% down conventional loans.
- **Competitive Financing** - Leverage owner-occupied loan rates for improved cash flow compared to investor loans.
- **Expanded Borrowing Capacity** - Access more than 10 traditional, fixed-rate 30-year mortgages.

The Nomad™ strategy has you:

1. Buy a property as an owner-occupant
2. Live there for a year
3. Then buy a new property
4. Convert the previous property to a rental
5. Repeat the process until you reach your financial goals

Nomad™ Variations

Let's explore the different variations of the Nomad™ strategy. Each offers unique advantages and approaches to real estate investing:

- **Traditional Nomad™** - This is the standard approach where you buy a property, live in it for a year, then rent it out and move to a new property. You repeat this process, building a portfolio of rental properties over time.

- **Fixer Upper Nomad™** - In this variation, you purchase properties that need some work. You live in the home while making improvements, potentially increasing its value before converting it into a rental.
- **Nomad™ by Proxy** - This strategy involves partnering with someone else who will live in the property. They qualify for the owner-occupied financing, so you don't have to move in.
- **Nomad™ to Short-Term Rental** - After living in the property, you convert it to a short-term rental instead of a long-term rental. This can potentially generate higher income and improve cash flow plus you get to live in a "vacation rental" for a year prior to converting it. Could also be a medium-term rental.
- **Nomad™ with House Hacking** - While living in the property, you rent out portions of it—like spare rooms or a basement apartment—to offset your living expenses and mortgage payments.
- **Nomad™ with Lease-Option Exit** - In this approach, when you're ready to move out, you offer the property as a rent-to-own opportunity instead of just a rental. This likely leads to improved cash flow, reduced sales costs and can—in many cases—provide you the down payment you need to buy your next property. This strategy can allow you to acquire a portfolio of rental properties with just a single down payment—which actually could be 0% down for your first purchase.
- **The Ultimate Real Estate Agent Retirement Plan™** - This variation is specifically for real estate agents. You use your commissions as part or all of your down payments (or discounts) when buying Nomad™

properties, building a real estate portfolio that can provide retirement income.

Financing Nomad™

When it comes to financing your Nomad™ properties, you have several options available.

Most Common Financing

When financing Nomad™ properties you're most likely to utilize traditional owner-occupant loans.

- **Nothing Down Options** - United States Department of Agriculture (USDA) and Veterans Affairs (VA) loans offer 0% down payment options for eligible borrowers. USDA has some rental restrictions making it less than ideal for Nomading™.
- **Low Down Payment Options** - Conventional loans with as little as 3% for first-time home buyers or, more commonly, 5% down payments, and Federal Housing Administration (FHA) loans with 3.5% down are available. These—especially the 5% down conventional loans—are the most common loans used by Nomads™.

With down payments less than 20%, you'll typically need to pay Private Mortgage Insurance (PMI). While this adds to your monthly costs, it allows you to start building your real estate portfolio sooner.

More Unusual Methods

While traditional owner-occupant loans are the most common financing method for Nomad™ properties, there are some less conventional approaches you might consider.

- **Larger Down Payment Conventional Financing** - Sometimes, putting more money down can be advantageous. You might secure a lower interest rate, avoid Private Mortgage Insurance (PMI), or improve your debt-to-income ratio.
- **Creative Financing Options** - One interesting creative financing possibility is loan assumption. If you find a property with an assumable mortgage at a favorable rate, you could take over the existing loan. This can be especially valuable in a high-interest-rate environment where interest rates have been lower recently.
- **Lease-Option Exits** - When you're ready to move to your next property, instead of simply renting out the previous one, you offer a lease-option to a tenant-buyer. Their non-refundable option fee can serve as the down payment (or partial down payment) for your next Nomad™ purchase. It's like having the previous property provide the down payment for your next property.
- **Fixer Upper Loans** - There are special loan programs like the FHA 203(k) loan program as one example that allow you to borrow money to make improvements to the property as part of your mortgage.

Holding

Traditional Nomad™ is generally considered a neutral to slightly active real estate investing strategy.

You're moving annually, which requires more effort than a typical buy-and-hold strategy, but it's not as intensive as, let's say, flipping houses.

Some variations of Nomad™ are a little more active than others.

For example:

- **Fixer Upper Nomad™** - More active than traditional Nomad™. You're not just moving, but also managing renovations and improvements.
- **Nomad™ by Proxy** – Slightly less active than traditional Nomad™. You're partnering with someone else who lives in the property, reducing some of your direct involvement. But you're also partnering with someone which can make it slightly more active in that way.
- **Nomad™ to Short-Term Rental** - Significantly more active. Managing short-term rentals typically requires more work than long-term rentals in exchange for significantly higher income from the property.
- **Nomad™ with House Hacking** - More active than traditional Nomad™. You're managing tenants or roommates while living in the property.
- **Nomad™ with Lease-Option Exit** - Slightly more active. You'll need to manage the lease-option

© 2024 James Orr. All rights reserved.

agreement and potentially work more closely with your tenant-buyer. But maintenance tends to be a little less with a tenant-buyer with ownership mentality than a tenant with renter mentality.

- **The Ultimate Real Estate Agent Retirement Plan**™ - More active, as you're combining your real estate agent duties with Nomad™ investing.

Duration

Most Nomads™ tend to be long-term buy and hold investors and therefore hold onto their properties forever.

However, your approach may evolve as your investment journey progresses.

Some Nomad™ investors choose to leverage their equity to improve returns or take larger positions in the market.

This is especially common with *Fixer Upper Nomad*™, where you might be tempted to utilize the forced appreciation you've captured through renovations.

As you approach retirement, you might find yourself adjusting your strategy.

For example, some investors—including Nomad™ investors—buy more properties than they ultimately need and then simplify their portfolio as they near retirement.

This could mean:

- Completely exiting real estate investing

- Reducing your portfolio to fewer, but better cash-flowing properties
- Shifting to less active investments that require less hands-on management

Exit Channels

While the Nomad™ strategy is designed for long-term holding, there may be situations where you decide to sell a property.

Here are the main exit channels you might consider:

- **Multiple Listing Service (MLS)** - This is the most common method for selling properties. You'll list your property with a real estate agent, who will market it to a wide audience of potential buyers. The MLS can help you reach more potential buyers, potentially leading to faster sales and better prices.
- **For Sale By Owner (FSBO)** - If you're comfortable handling the sale process yourself, you might choose to sell your property without an agent. This can save you on commission fees, but it requires more time and effort on your part. You'll need to market the property, handle showings, and navigate the legal aspects of the sale.
- **Auctions** - While less common for individual properties, auctions can be an effective way to sell quickly. They create a sense of urgency among buyers and can sometimes result in higher prices due to competitive bidding. However, they also come with the risk of selling below market value if bidding is low.

- **Lease-Option Exit** - This is particularly relevant for the Nomad™ with Lease-Option Exit variation. You offer your tenant the option to buy the property at a predetermined price. This can be attractive as it may allow you to sell without incurring real estate agent sales commissions, and your tenant-buyer is already familiar with the property.

While not a marketing channel itself, utilizing a 1031 tax deferred exchange allows you to defer capital gains taxes and depreciation recapture taxes by reinvesting the proceeds into another "like-kind" property. It's a great way to upgrade your portfolio without a hefty tax bill.

Check out *Should I Sell My Rental Property?* in *The Real Estate Investing Mentor* series for more information on the calculations and considerations for selling rental properties.

Exit Financing

When it comes to selling your Nomad™ property, you have several options for how your buyers might finance the purchase.

They include:

- **Never Sell** - This is actually a common approach for many Nomad™ investors. You might choose to hold onto your properties indefinitely, benefiting from long-term appreciation and rental income.
- **Traditional Owner-Occupant Loans** - If you're selling to someone who plans to live in the property, they might use conventional financing, FHA, USDA or VA loans.

These often come with lower down payments and better interest rates, making your property more accessible to a wider range of buyers.

- **Traditional Non-Owner-Occupant Loans** - When selling to an investor, they'll likely use investment property loans. These typically require higher down payments (often 20-25%) and come with slightly higher interest rates.
- **Cash** - Some buyers, especially investors, might offer to purchase your property with cash. While this can lead to a quicker, smoother transaction, cash buyers often expect a discount on the purchase price.
- **Rent-to-Own Transition** - Although not typical, you could consider transitioning to a rent-to-own arrangement. This allows you to exit more slowly and potentially minimize fees. It can be particularly useful if you're using the *Nomad™ with Lease-Option Exit* variation.

Investor/Entrepreneur

First, what's the difference between a real estate investor and a real estate entrepreneur?

- Real Estate Investors tend to invest money with the hope of getting a return on that money.
- Real Estate Entrepreneurs tend to invest their time—and maybe a little bit of money—with the hope of getting a return on their time and money.

So, where does each variation of Nomad™ typically fall on that continuum?

- **Traditional Nomad™** - This leans more towards the investor side. You're primarily investing money with the hope of getting a return, although living in the house for a year does require more active involvement than traditional buy and hold.
- **Fixer Upper Nomad™** - This variation shifts more towards the real estate entrepreneur side. You're not just investing money, but also time and effort into renovations.
- **Nomad™ by Proxy** - This strategy is more investor-focused. While you're still orchestrating the process, someone else is living in the property, reducing your direct time investment.
- **Nomad™ to Short-Term Rental** - This is decidedly more entrepreneurial. Managing short-term rentals requires more time and effort, but can potentially yield higher returns.
- **Nomad™ with House Hacking** - This falls somewhere in the middle. You're investing money, but also actively managing tenants or roommates while living in the property.
- **Nomad™ with Lease-Option Exit** - This leans towards the Real Estate Entrepreneur side. You're not just investing money, but also structuring deals and potentially working more closely with your tenant-buyers.
- **The Ultimate Real Estate Agent Retirement Plan™** - This variation leans more towards the real estate entrepreneur side. As a real estate agent, you're actively using your professional skills to facilitate your own property purchases. By combining your expertise in real

estate transactions with Nomad™ investing principles, you're strategically leveraging your time, knowledge, and commissions to build a robust investment portfolio and maximize your long-term returns.

Money Required

One of the advantages of Nomad™ is that you can do the strategy with little or no down payments.

What's common and what's less common for money required?

Most Common

Here are the common money requirements:

- **Down Payment** - You'll need 0% (for VA or USDA loans), 3% (for some first-time home buyer conventional loans), 3.5% (for FHA loans), or 5% (for most conventional loans) of the purchase price. Although USDA loans are much more difficult to utilize because of the rental restrictions.
- **Closing Costs** - These typically range from 2% to 5% of the purchase price and include fees for appraisal, title insurance, and loan origination.
- **Rent Ready Costs** - Budget for minor repairs or upgrades to make the property tenant-ready when you convert it to a rental. This can vary widely but might be around $1,000 to $5,000. But could be a lot more if

you're doing *Fixer Upper Nomad™* or *Nomad™ to Short-Term Rentals*.

- **Living Costs** - You'll have these whether you do Nomad™ or not, but factor in your personal living expenses for at least a year while you occupy the property. They may be slightly higher than if you weren't Nomading™ in some cases like when you buy a more expenses house to Nomad™ in then you would otherwise live in if you weren't Nomading™.
- **Cumulative Negative Cash Flow** - Due to low initial down payments, you might experience negative cash flow initially. If you had put more down, you wouldn't have negative cash flow. So, negative cash flow is effectively a deferred down payment, financing a portion over time. *Cumulative Negative Cash Flow* is the total amount of negative cash flow you're estimating you'll have before the rents increase enough where you no longer have negative cash flow. This *Cumulative Negative Cash Flow* is usually less than what you'd need to put down in additional down payment to have positive cash flow upfront. Setting aside this amount when you first invest is a more conservative approach. Be prepared to cover this shortfall until rents increase enough to eliminate the negative cash flow.
- **Reserves** - You should aim for at least 6 months of mortgage payments and other operating expenses as a safety net.

Remember, these costs can vary based on your specific Nomad™ variation and local market conditions.

14

Less Common

While the common scenarios for Nomad™ investing typically involve traditional down payments and financing, there are less common situations where the money required can vary significantly:

- **Nomad™ by Proxy** – If you're the one moving into the properties as the proxy, you might need little to no money upfront. Someone else provides the down payment while you're the one moving in. This can significantly reduce your initial investment.
- **Nomad™ with Lease-Option Exit** - You could potentially use non-refundable deposits from lease-option agreements on properties you're moving out of as down payments for your next Nomad™ property. This creative financing approach can reduce the amount of new money you need to bring to the table.
- **The Ultimate Real Estate Agent Retirement Plan™** - As a real estate agent using this strategy, you might benefit from commission rebates on your purchases, effectively reducing your down payment requirements.
- **Higher Down Payments or All-Cash Purchases** - While less common in the Nomad™ strategy, putting more money down or buying properties outright with cash is an option if you have the funds available. This can lead to better cash flow from the start but requires more upfront capital.
- **Nomad™ to Short-Term Rental** - This variation might allow you to put down a 10% down payment for a second home. This unique scenario could enable you to

purchase two properties in the same year, accelerating your portfolio growth. Also, realize that *Rent Ready Costs* for short-term rentals tends to be significantly higher than other variations of Nomad™ as you'll need to prepare the property as a short-term rental.

- **Fixer Upper Nomad™** - When pursuing this strategy, you'll need to budget for renovation costs. The amount can vary widely depending on the property's condition and your planned improvements. You might consider options like FHA 203(k) loans, which allow you to finance both the purchase and renovation costs in a single loan.

Credit Required

When it comes to credit requirements for the Nomad™ strategy, you'll typically need to qualify for traditional owner-occupant financing.

That's because you are moving into the property; failing to move in could be considered loan fraud. You will sign a document from the lender at closing stating you intend to occupy the property.

Most lenders require a minimum credit score of 620 for Nomad™ investors.

However, FHA or VA loans may allow credit scores as low as 580.

You may want to put in the effort to improve your credit score since better credit scores often lead to more favorable interest rates and lower Private Mortgage Insurance (PMI) costs which can lead to improved cash flow.

These are some less common credit situations:

- If you're buying a property with cash, your credit score won't be a factor
- In a Nomad™ by Proxy scenario, where someone else is obtaining the loan, you may not need to qualify personally

Remember, your credit score is just one piece of the puzzle. Lenders will also consider your income, debt-to-income ratio, and employment history when deciding whether to approve your loan.

IMPORTANT NOTE: Credit requirements can change over time. It's always best to check with your local lender for the most up-to-date information on credit requirements.

Skills Required

The Nomad™ real estate investing strategy requires a unique set of skills to execute successfully.

Let's break down the primary skills you'll need:

- **Deal Analysis** - You'll need to evaluate properties thoroughly, considering factors like purchase price, potential rental income, and long-term appreciation. This skill is crucial for making informed investment decisions.
- **Find Cash Flowing Deals** - Identifying properties that will generate positive cash flow—or at least minimal

negative cash flow for the no or low downpayment—is essential.

- **Acquisition Financing** - Understanding various financing options, particularly owner-occupant loans, is a key skill. You'll need to navigate the mortgage process and maintain good credit, strong income and relatively low expenses to qualify for multiple properties over time.
- **Property Management** - Whether you're managing properties yourself or hiring a company, you'll need to understand the basics of tenant screening, maintenance, and local landlord-tenant laws.

Now, let's look at the additional skills required for each Nomad™ variation:

- **Fixer Upper Nomad™** - You'll need basic home improvement skills or the ability to manage contractors. Understanding renovation costs and potential return on investment is another important skill for this variation.
- **Nomad™ by Proxy** - This requires strong communication and coordination skills to manage the relationship.
- **Nomad™ to Short-Term Rental** - You'll need to understand short-term rental regulations, pricing strategies, and guest management. Marketing skills are also important to keep your property booked.
- **Nomad™ with House Hacking** - This variation requires good interpersonal skills for living with tenants or roommates.

- **Nomad™ with Lease-Option Exit** - You'll need to understand lease-option agreements and be skilled in negotiating with potential tenant-buyers.
- **The Ultimate Real Estate Agent Retirement Plan™** - This strategy requires a real estate license and leverages an agent's skills at buying properties.

Stability

Shane Parrish's concept of active versus passive stability is particularly relevant to real estate investing. Let's explore how it applies to your Nomad™ journey.

In real estate, most strategies, including Nomad™, are actively stable. This means you'll need to put in consistent effort to keep your investments performing well.

Some Nomad™ variations require even more active involvement:

- **Fixer Upper Nomad™** - You're not just living in the property, but actively improving it. This requires more hands-on effort and management.
- **Nomad™ to Short-Term Rental** - This variation demands frequent tenant turnover management, cleaning, and constant marketing. It's a more intensive, day-to-day involvement.
- **Nomad™ with Lease-Option Exit** - Here, you're not just managing a property, but also structuring deals with potential future buyers. This requires ongoing coordination with your tenant-buyers, sales and then re-

investment when tenant-buyers opt to buy your properties.

Scalability

The Nomad™ strategy offers a unique approach to scaling your real estate portfolio by purchasing owner-occupant properties with no or low down payments and sequentially buying properties each year as you convert your previous ones to rentals

Here's how scalable it can be:

- **Acquisition Speed** - Nomad™ is typically limited to one property per year, which can slow down scaling compared to other strategies.
- **Accelerating Acquisition** - You can potentially increase your acquisition speed through:

  o *Nomad™ by Proxy* with other people
  o *Nomad™ to Short-Term Rental*, allowing a 10% down payment on a second home in parallel
  o Combining Nomad™ with non-owner-occupant strategies like traditional buy and hold real estate investing

- **Lower Down Payments** - Nomad™ typically requires about 1/4 of the down payment compared to traditional buy and hold (5% vs 20%). This makes it easier to scale from a capital perspective.
- **Better Financing Terms** - Owner-occupant interest rates are often more favorable, improving your debt-to-income ratio. This can make it easier to qualify for loans

and improve cash flow for saving future down payments. However, the lower down payments can work against this.

- **Lease-Option Exits** - Using lease-option exits could potentially eliminate the need for down payments on future properties. This strategy optimizes your return on equity as you sell to tenant-buyers and reinvest the proceeds.

If you your limiting factor scaling was being able to save for down payments then the Nomad™ strategy may be a great scaling solution for achieving your real estate investing goals.

Risk Exposure

While the Nomad™ strategy offers many benefits, it's important to understand the potential risks involved.

Overall, Nomad™ has a medium risk rating.

Let's break down the key risk factors present when Nomading:

- **Amplified Returns** - Small down payments can lead to amplified returns, both positive and negative. This means your potential gains could be higher, but so could your losses.
- **Increased Likelihood of Negative Cash Flow** - With smaller down payments, you're more likely to experience negative cash flow, especially in the early years. This is essentially a form of deferred down

payment. If you put enough down, you wouldn't have negative cash flow.

- **Market Volatility** - You're exposed to the risk of price declines during ownership, which could impact your equity position. This is like other strategies with long holding durations.
- **Rent Fluctuations** - There's a risk of rent decline during ownership, which could affect your cash flow and overall returns. This is also like other strategies with long holding durations.
- **Credit Risk** - Your credit is at stake with each property you finance. Late payments or defaults could significantly impact your credit score.
- **Property Management Challenges** - You'll face typical tenant and property management risks, including potential property damage, vacancies, and maintenance issues.

Some Nomad™ variations come with additional risks:

- **Fixer Upper Nomad™** - You're exposed to renovation risks, including unexpected costs and potential delays.
- **Nomad™ to Short-Term Rental** - While potentially more profitable, this variation carries slightly higher risks due to changing local regulations, HOA rules, and insurance policies for short-term rentals.
- **Nomad™ with House Hacking** - This strategy involves living with tenants, which could lead to personal conflicts or privacy issues.
- **Nomad™ with Lease-Option Exit** - There's a risk that tenant-buyers may not exercise their option, requiring

you to find a new tenant-buyer. This is often offset by collecting another non-refundable option fee from the new tenant-buyer.

Remember, while these risks exist, many can be mitigated through careful planning, thorough due diligence, and proper management.

Profit Speed

When it comes to real estate investing, understanding the speed at which you can generate profits is important.

Let's break down the 4 primary returns you can expect from your Nomad™ investment property:

- **Appreciation** - The increase in your property's value over time.
- **Cash Flow** - The monthly income you receive after covering all expenses.
- **Debt Paydown** - The reduction of your mortgage balance as your tenants essentially pay your loan.

- **Tax Benefits** - Advantages like depreciation deductions that can lower your tax liability generating extra cash in your pocket.

In addition, you have the return you earn on the reserves you've set aside for the property while it is in savings or invested in something else.

Now, let's dive into how quickly you can start seeing these returns with the Nomad™ strategy.

Speed of Returns

With Nomad™, you'll start benefiting from appreciation and debt paydown almost immediately. By purchasing your property, you're already building equity through these two returns.

Cash flow and tax benefits typically kick in after your first year, when you convert the property to a rental.

However, you may accelerate this timeline with house hacking; if you rent out part of your property while living there, you can start generating cash flow and *Cash Flow from Depreciation™* right away.

Keep in mind that using a property manager might slightly delay your cash flow slightly once you convert to a rental, but it can save you time and headaches in the long run.

Returns can also be delayed slightly if you utilize popular short-term rental platforms that delay payouts.

Size of Returns

The size of your returns is often calculated as a percentage of your initial investment. This is typically expressed as Cash on Cash Return on Investment (ROI) although some investors prefer to use a different calculation referred to as Capitalization Rate (Cap Rate).

Nomad™ Variations and Profit Speed

Different Nomad™ variations can affect your profit speed:

- **Traditional Nomad™** - Follows the standard timeline described above.
- **Fixer Upper Nomad™** - Improves equity through forced appreciation (fix up), but usually not accessible until you sell or refinance.
- **Nomad™ by Proxy** - Depending on how its structured could speed up returns.
- **Nomad™ to Short-Term Rental** - Typically like the standard timeline described above except the returns from short-term rental platforms may delay payouts briefly when you first start.
- **Nomad™ with House Hacking** - Allows for immediate cash flow through renting out portions of your living space.
- **Nomad™ with Lease-Option Exit** - Like the standard timeline above, except when you prepare to convert it to

a rent-to-own you front-load some of your profit with a non-refundable option fee from your tenant-buyer.

- **The Ultimate Real Estate Agent Retirement Plan™** - Can get an immediate rebate on your down payment from the commission you earned buying the property to live in.

Finding Deals

There are some common methods of finding Nomad™ deals and some less common, more unusual ways.

Let's look at both.

Most Common Methods

Here are some of the most common methods for finding Nomad™ properties:

- **Multiple Listing Service (MLS)** - This is often your go-to resource because it offers the largest selection of properties to choose from. The MLS provides a comprehensive database of properties listed by real estate agents. You can set up alerts for properties that match your criteria, making it easier to spot potential Nomad™ opportunities.
- **For Sale By Owner (FSBO)** - **Actively Marketed** - These are properties that owners are selling without the help of a real estate agent. You can find these listings on websites dedicated to FSBO properties and by driving around neighborhoods looking for "For Sale" signs.

- **FSBO - Hidden** - This category includes properties that aren't actively marketed but whose owners might be willing to sell. To uncover these hidden gems, you'll need to do some legwork:
  - **Marketing** - Send out mailers or run targeted ads in areas you're interested in. Your message could be something like, "We're looking to buy a home in your neighborhood. Are you thinking of selling?"
  - **Networking** - Talk to people in your target areas. Join local community groups, attend neighborhood events, or even strike up conversations. You never know who might be considering selling their property.

More Unusual Methods

One less common but potentially valuable way to find Nomad™ properties is through wholesalers. These are individuals or companies that find off-market properties and sell them to investors.

Wholesalers often have access to deals that aren't listed on the MLS. They may find motivated sellers or distressed properties that could be perfect for your Nomad™ strategy.

To connect with wholesalers:

- Attend local real estate investing meetups or networking events
- Join online real estate investing forums or social media groups

- Search online for "real estate wholesalers" in your target area

Remember, while wholesalers can provide unique opportunities, always do your due diligence. Verify property conditions, values, and potential returns before making any commitments.

Analyzing Deals

When analyzing Nomad™ properties, we highly recommend using *The World's Greatest Real Estate Deal Analysis Spreadsheet*™. This powerful tool is designed to work for all Nomad™ variations, making it an invaluable resource for your investment journey.

You can download this spreadsheet for free at:

https://REFP.com/spreadsheet

It's a comprehensive tool that allows you to input various property details and financial parameters to get a clear picture of your potential investment.

Here's why it's so useful:

- It allows you to analyze cash flow, appreciation, debt paydown and *Cash Flow from Depreciation*™ for each Nomad™ variation
- It shows you a variety of return on investment and return on equity calculations
- It allows you to track your investment performance over time—not just when you buy
- The spreadsheet is simple to use with its intuitive dashboard, but also extremely powerful with the ability to override just about any value for any year in the overrides tab
- It provides long-term projections, giving you a clear view of your investment's potential over time

Download the spreadsheet for free and use it to analyze your Nomad™ and other deals.

Market Conditions

When utilizing the Nomad™ strategy, market conditions play an important role in your success.

Let's explore both ideal and challenging market conditions to help you make informed decisions.

Ideal Market Conditions

In the best-case scenario, you'll want to look for markets that offer:

- **Strong Cash Flow Potential** - These markets allow you to generate positive cash flow from the start, even with a smaller down payment.
- **Healthy Property Appreciation** - Look for areas where property values are steadily increasing over time. This helps build your equity faster.
- **Healthy Rent Appreciation** - Markets where rents are rising can boost your cash flow and overall returns.
- **High Demand for Rentals** - Areas with a strong rental market can help ensure consistent occupancy and income.
- **Favorable Local Regulations** - Some markets have landlord-friendly laws that can make property management easier especially short-term rental regulations if you're utilizing that Nomad™ variation. Plus, markets that encourage lease-options if you're utilizing that Nomad™ variation.

Challenging Market Conditions

On the flip side, some market conditions can make the Nomad™ strategy more difficult:

- **Significant Negative Cash Flow** - Markets where properties consistently produce negative cash flow, even with reasonable down payments, can make it more challenging to Nomad™.

- **Stagnant or Declining Property Values** - Areas with no appreciation or even negative appreciation can hinder your long-term wealth-building goals.
- **Stagnant or Declining Rents** - If rents aren't keeping pace with inflation or are declining, it can impact your cash flow and returns.
- **Oversaturated Rental Markets** - Too much competition can lead to higher vacancy rates and lower rents.
- **Strict Local Regulations** - Some areas have laws that make it challenging to be a landlord, do short-term rentals, or lease-options. This potentially increasing your costs and risks or, in some cases, limits your ability to utilize your preferred Nomad™ strategy variation at all.

Remember, no market is perfect, and conditions can change over time.

Your success with the Nomad™ strategy often depends on your ability to navigate less-than-ideal market conditions effectively.

Accessibility/Availability

The accessibility and availability of Nomad™ properties can vary depending on market conditions and your specific situation:

- In many markets, you'll find plenty of suitable properties listed on the MLS, giving you a wide selection to choose from.
- Some markets may require more careful sifting and sorting to identify the best deals that align with your Nomad™ strategy.
- Challenging markets might make it difficult to find positive cash-flowing properties, especially if you're planning smaller down payments. In these cases, you might need to consider deferred down payments in the form of initial negative cash flow or utilizing all the strategies we discuss for improving cash flow included in as a bonus chapter of this book.

Interest rates play a significant role in determining whether properties will cash flow.

Owner-occupant rates can provide an advantage over traditional buy and hold strategies helping improve cash flow.

Using Retirement Account

While you typically can't use self-directed retirement accounts directly for Nomad™ properties due to living in the property, there are two alternative approaches to consider.

- If you have a Self-Directed 401k, you could borrow the money from your Self-Directed 401k to buy a property.
- If the returns are good enough, you could choose to pay the penalty and liquidate some of your retirement funds to use for Nomading™.

First, if you have a Self-Directed 401k, you could borrow the money from your Self-Directed 401k to buy a property. There are limits to this, but it is possible to borrow money from yourself and this money could be used to buy an owner-occupant property (or several owner-occupant properties).

This option is not available for self-directed IRAs.

Second, you could potentially access your retirement funds by paying the associated penalties and taxes to use them for a Nomad™ investment.

Self-directed IRAs and 401(k)s are designed for investment purposes only, and living in a property owned by your retirement account is considered a prohibited transaction. However, if you choose to withdraw funds from your retirement account, you could use them for a Nomad™ property.

This strategy might be worthwhile since the returns on Nomad™ properties tend to be very high. The potential gains from your Nomad™ investment could outweigh the penalties and taxes incurred from early withdrawal. However, it's crucial to carefully run the numbers and consider all factors before making this decision.

BONUS CHAPTERS

Introduction to Real Estate Deal Analysis

Analyzing real estate deals can be a daunting task, but with the right tools and knowledge, it becomes much more manageable. One powerful tool we recommend is *The World's Greatest Real Estate Deal Analysis Spreadsheet™*. This spreadsheet is designed to help you evaluate the financial viability of real estate investments with ease and precision.

In our book, *How to Analyze Real Estate Deals*, we delve deep into the intricacies of deal analysis, providing step-by-step instructions and expert insights. This introduction aims to give you a high-level overview of the process and how to effectively use the spreadsheet to make informed investment decisions.

The spreadsheet allows you to input various data points such as purchase price, mortgage details, monthly income, and annual expenses. It then performs complex calculations to provide you with key metrics like cash flow, return on investment (ROI), and internal rate of return (IRR).

By leveraging this tool, you can:

- Quickly assess the profitability of potential deals.
- Compare multiple investment opportunities.
- Make data-driven decisions to maximize your returns.

Whether you're a seasoned investor or just starting out, understanding how to analyze real estate deals is crucial for success.

Download Spreadsheet for Free

Unlock the full potential of your real estate investments by downloading *The World's Greatest Real Estate Deal Analysis Spreadsheet*™ for free.

Get your copy at: https://REFP.info/spreadsheet

We recommend always keeping an unedited, fresh copy on your hard drive in case you can't download the spreadsheet in the future.

Before analyzing a property, always make a new copy.

Spreadsheet Inputs

Entering the inputs into the spreadsheet is simple. Here's what you need to know:

- The manila fields indicate where you should input your data.
- The gray background with blue text shows the calculations that are automatically performed for you.

First, please name the deal that you're analyzing in the field just above the "Purchase Inputs". This will allow you to know which deal you're looking at if you're considering analyzing multiple deals or one deal multiple ways.

Purchase Inputs

Before we dive into the specifics of analyzing a real estate deal, let's go over the inputs required for the spreadsheet. These inputs will be divided into two columns: one for percentages and one for dollar amounts (or numbers).

Understanding what to enter in each field is crucial for accurately analyzing your deal. Let's go over what to put in each field next.

- **ARV** - Enter the After Repair Value, which is the estimated value of the property after all repairs and improvements have been made.
- **Purchase Price** - Enter the amount you are paying to acquire the property from the seller.
- **Seller Concessions** - Enter any financial concessions or incentives that the seller has agreed to provide, such as covering closing costs or offering repair credits.
- **Down Payment** - Enter the initial amount you will pay out-of-pocket towards the purchase of the property. Be sure to check out our guide on creative ways to come up with down payments for rental properties.
- **Closing Costs** - Enter the total costs associated with closing the real estate transaction, including title insurance, attorney fees, and other related expenses.
- **Rent Ready Costs** - Enter the expenses required to make the property ready for tenants, such as cleaning, repairs, and any necessary upgrades.
- **Cumulative Negative Cash Flow** - If you have negative cash flow enter the total cumulative amount of negative cash flow you anticipate before the property becomes cash flow positive. We recommend you set this aside to reduce risk. You may also want to check out our book on *How to Improve Cash Flow on Rental Properties* to get rid of negative cash flow on your properties.
- **Total Invested** - This is calculated for you. It is the cumulative amount of money you have invested in the

property, including **Down Payment, Closing Costs, Rent Ready Costs, Cumulative Negative Cash Flow,** minus any **Seller Concessions** you received from the seller.

Mortgage Inputs

To accurately analyze your real estate deal, it's essential to input detailed information about your mortgage and financing. These inputs will help calculate your monthly payments, interest costs, and overall financial commitment. Here's what you'll need to enter:

- **Mortgage Amount** - This is calculated for you. It is the total amount of money you are borrowing to finance the purchase of the property.
- **Mortgage Interest Rate** - Enter the annual interest rate for your mortgage. This is the percentage of the loan amount that you will pay as interest each year.
- **Loan Term** - Enter the duration of your mortgage loan in months. 360 months is a 30-year loan. This is the period over which you will repay the loan.
- **Private Mortgage Insurance** - Enter the monthly cost of private mortgage insurance (PMI) if applicable. PMI is typically required if your down payment is less than 20% of the purchase price. If you don't have PMI, use 0.000% here.
- **Drop PMI LTV** - Enter the loan-to-value (LTV) ratio at which PMI will be dropped. This is the point at which your equity in the property is high enough that PMI is no

longer required. If you don't have PMI, use 0.000% here.

Monthly Income

Accurately estimating your monthly income is critical for assessing the profitability of your real estate investment. This section will guide you through the necessary inputs for calculating your expected monthly income from the property, including rent and any additional sources of income.

- **Monthly Rent** - Enter the amount of rent you expect to receive from tenants each month. If you don't know how to determine what rent is on a property you're considering, you might want to check out our book on *How to Determine Rent Comps*.
- **Monthly Other Income** - Enter any additional monthly income from the property, such as parking fees, laundry services, or storage rentals.

Annual Expenses

Understanding and accurately estimating annual expenses is crucial for analyzing the financial viability of a real estate investment. This section will guide you through the various costs associated with owning and maintaining a property, from vacancy rates to property taxes and insurance. By thoroughly accounting for each of these expenses, you can better predict your investment's profitability and make more informed decisions.

- **Vacancy Rate** - Enter the percentage of time the property is expected to be vacant each year.
- **Property Taxes** - Enter the annual property tax amount you will pay for owning the property.
- **Property Insurance** - Enter the annual cost of insuring the property.
- **HOA Dues** - Enter the annual homeowner association fees, if applicable.
- **Utilities** - Enter the annual cost of utilities that you will pay as the property owner.
- **Other Expenses 1 and 2** - Enter any other annual expenses not covered in the previous categories.
- **Maintenance** - Enter the annual cost of maintaining the property, including repairs and routine upkeep.
- **CapEx** - Enter the annual amount set aside for capital expenditures. Consider our book and spreadsheet on CapEx for more guidance.
- **Management** - Enter the annual cost of property management services, if applicable.

Depreciation Details

Depreciation is a critical aspect of real estate investment analysis, as it allows you to account for the gradual reduction in the value of your property over time. Properly calculating and understanding depreciation can provide significant tax benefits and improve the overall financial picture of your investment. This section will guide you through the necessary inputs for determining depreciation, including land value, property type, and your effective income tax rate. By accurately inputting these details, you can optimize your investment strategy and maximize potential returns.

- **Land Value** - Enter the percent of the property that represents the value of the land. This value is used to calculate depreciation.
- **Property Type (C or R)** - Indicate whether the property is classified as commercial (C) or residential (R). This affects the depreciation schedule.
- **Effective Income Tax Rate** - Enter your effective income tax rate. This rate is used to estimate the tax benefits of depreciation.

Overrides

The spreadsheet is designed to be user-friendly on the Dashboard, while offering extensive functionality in the Overrides section. This dual approach ensures that users can easily navigate and input basic data, but also have access to more advanced features when needed.

In the Overrides tab, you have the ability to:

- **Modify any other inputs** - Adjust various parameters to suit your specific needs and scenarios.
- **Perform custom calculations** - Create and implement your own unique calculations to gain deeper insights into your investments.

- **View intermediate calculations** - Access detailed breakdowns of the calculations that drive the final results, providing transparency and better understanding.
- **Analyze performance over an extended period** - The spreadsheet allows you to conduct analysis through up to 40 years, enabling long-term strategic planning.
- **Track investment performance** - Use the Overrides tab to monitor how your investment evolves over time, making it easier to adjust your strategy as needed.

This comprehensive functionality ensures that the spreadsheet is not only a powerful tool for initial analysis but also a valuable resource for ongoing management and optimization of your real estate investments.

Dashboard

The Dashboard section provides a comprehensive overview of your real estate investment's key metrics and financial performance.

Here, you can quickly assess your monthly cash flow, return on investment (ROI), internal rate of return (IRR), and other critical indicators.

The Dashboard is designed to offer a user-friendly summary of your investment, allowing you to make informed decisions and track your progress over time.

Of course, you can dig into the Overrides tab for a ridiculous amount of additional detail.

Monthly Cash Flow - Year 1

This chart displays the Monthly Cash Flow, *Cash Flow from Depreciation*™, and the combined total, referred to as *True Cash Flow*™.

Understanding these metrics is crucial as they provide a comprehensive view of your investment's financial health.

- Monthly Cash Flow shows the actual cash inflow and outflow.
- *Cash Flow from Depreciation*™ accounts for tax benefits derived from property depreciation.
- *True Cash Flow*™ combines these figures, offering a more accurate representation of your investment's profitability.

Return in Dollars - Year 1

This chart displays the estimated dollars earned from your real estate investment over the first year, including Appreciation, Cash Flow, *Cash Flow from Depreciation*™, and Debt Paydown.

Understanding these metrics provides a holistic view of your investment's performance:

- **Appreciation** - Reflects the increase in property value over the year.
- **Cash Flow** - Shows the actual cash inflow and outflow.
- ***Cash Flow from Depreciation***™ - Accounts for tax benefits derived from property depreciation.

44

- **Debt Paydown** - Indicates the amount of principal paid down on your mortgage over the year.

Additionally, the chart includes earnings on reserves:

- **6 Months of Reserves in Savings** - Illustrates the interest earned if you set aside 6 months of reserves in a savings account.
- **Most of 12 Months of Reserves in Another Investment** - Shows the potential earnings if most of 12 months of reserves are invested in another investment vehicle like the stock market.

These combined figures provide a comprehensive representation of your investment's profitability and financial health over the first year.

You can see the totals at the bottom of the chart.

Return on Investment - Year 1

This chart displays the return on investment (ROI) from your real estate investment over the first year, including Appreciation, Cash Flow, *Cash Flow from Depreciation*™, and Debt Paydown.

Understanding these metrics provides a holistic view of your investment's performance:

- **Appreciation** - Reflects the increase in property value over the year divided by the total amount invested (and reserves where applicable).

- **Cash Flow** - Shows the actual cash inflow and outflow divided by the total amount invested (and reserves where applicable).
- *Cash Flow from Depreciation*™ - Accounts for tax benefits derived from property depreciation divided by the total amount invested (and reserves where applicable).
- **Debt Paydown** - Indicates the amount of principal paid down on your mortgage over the year divided by the total amount invested (and reserves where applicable).

Additionally, the chart includes ROI on reserves:

- **6 Months of Reserves in Savings** - Illustrates the interest earned if you set aside 6 months of reserves in a savings account, divided by the total amount invested plus 6 months of reserves.
- **Most of 12 Months of Reserves in Another Investment** - Shows the potential earnings if most of 12 months of reserves are invested in another investment vehicle like the stock market, divided by the total amount invested plus 12 months of reserves.

These combined figures provide a comprehensive representation of your investment's profitability and financial health over the first year in terms of ROI.

You can see the totals at the bottom of the chart.

46

Returns if Sold (ROI and IRR)

This chart illustrates the return on investment if you sold the property each year for the first 20 years. It includes three key metrics:

- **Simple Annualized Return on Investment** - This metric shows the average annual return on your investment, calculated by dividing the total return by the number of years you held the property.
- **Compound Annualized Return on Investment** - This metric accounts for the compounding effect, showing the average annual return on your investment when considering the reinvestment of earnings.
- **Internal Rate of Return (IRR)** - This metric represents the annualized rate of return that makes the net present value (NPV) of all cash flows (both inflows and outflows) from the investment equal to zero.

These metrics provide a comprehensive view of the financial performance of your investment over time, helping you to understand the potential long-term profitability and compare it with other investment opportunities.

Cash on Cash ROI & Cap Rate - Years 1-5

This chart displays the Cash on Cash Return on Investment (ROI) and the Capitalization Rate (Cap Rate) for the property over the first 5 years.

Understanding these metrics provides a comprehensive view of your investment's performance:

- **Cash on Cash ROI** - This metric shows the annual return on your investment based on the actual cash invested. It is calculated by dividing the annual pre-tax cash flow by the total cash invested.
- **Cap Rate** - This metric represents the annual return on the property based on its current market value. It is calculated by dividing the net operating income (NOI) by the property's current market value.

By understanding these metrics, you can gauge the effectiveness and profitability of your investment, enabling you to make well-informed decisions and evaluate it against other potential investment opportunities.

Return on True Net Equity™

This chart shows you the returns you're earning from Appreciation, Cash Flow, *Cash Flow from Depreciation*™, and Debt Paydown divided by the equity minus the costs to access that equity with a sale (what we call True Net Equity™). It shows the first 20 years. It also shows the total of all four areas of return.

Understanding these metrics is crucial for assessing the true profitability of your real estate investment:

- **Appreciation** - Reflects the increase in property value over the year.
- **Cash Flow** - Shows the actual cash inflow and outflow.

- **Cash Flow from Depreciation**™ - Accounts for tax benefits derived from property depreciation.
- **Debt Paydown** - Indicates the amount of principal paid down on your mortgage over the year.

By dividing these returns by the True Net Equity™, you get a more accurate representation of your investment's performance, considering the costs to access the equity. This comprehensive view helps in making informed decisions and comparing the potential returns of different investments.

For more information on True Net Equity™ consider checking out our books about that:

- Should I Sell My Rental My Rental Property?
- Should I Sell My Refinance My Rental Property?

Annual Key Metrics - Year 1

This chart displays the financial performance of your real estate investment in terms of Gross Potential Income (GPI), Gross Operating Income (GOI), Operating Expenses (OpEx), and Net Operating Income (NOI) for the first year.

Understanding these metrics provides a comprehensive view of your investment's revenue and profitability:

- **Gross Potential Income (GPI)** - This metric represents the total income the property could generate if it were fully rented and all units were occupied at market rent rates, without accounting for any vacancies or losses.

- **Gross Operating Income (GOI)** - This metric reflects the actual income received from the property, including rent and other income sources, after accounting for vacancies and any collection losses.
- **Operating Expenses (OpEx)** - These are the costs associated with maintaining and managing the property, excluding mortgage payments and capital expenditures.
- **Net Operating Income (NOI)** - This metric is calculated by subtracting the operating expenses from the Gross Operating Income. It represents the income generated by the property after all operating expenses have been deducted.

By understanding these metrics, you can better assess the financial health and profitability of your real estate investment, helping you make more strategic decisions and compare it with other investment opportunities.

Annual Non-Loan Expenses - Year 1

This chart displays the financial performance of your real estate investment by itemizing all the non-loan expenses for the first year. Understanding these metrics provides a comprehensive view of your property's operational costs, which are crucial for accurate financial analysis and planning:

- **Vacancy Rate** - The percentage of time the property is expected to be vacant each year.
- **Property Taxes** - The annual amount paid for property taxes.

- **Property Insurance** - The cost of insuring the property for the year.
- **HOA Dues** - Annual homeowner association fees, if applicable.
- **Utilities** - The total annual cost of utilities paid by the property owner.
- **Other Expenses 1 and 2** - Any additional annual expenses not covered in the previous categories.
- **Maintenance** - The annual expense for maintaining the property, including routine repairs and upkeep.
- **CapEx** - The annual amount set aside for capital expenditures, such as major repairs or replacements.
- **Management Fees** - The cost of property management services, if utilized.

By breaking down these non-loan expenses, this chart helps you understand the total operational costs associated with your property, enabling you to better manage your investment and forecast its financial performance.

Equities and Cost-To-Access

This chart displays the equity in your real estate deal each year for the first 20 years, focusing on two key metrics: *True Net Equity*™ and Cash-Out Refi Equity.

- ***True Net Equity*™** - This is the equity minus the costs to access it through a sale. It shows the real profit after considering selling costs.

- **Cash-Out Refi Equity** - This is the equity available if you refinance the property. It helps you understand the potential funds available through refinancing.
- **Cost-To-Access Equity Percentages** - The chart also shows the costs (as a percentage of the equity) associated with accessing each type of equity. This provides insight into the expenses involved.

Understanding these metrics is crucial for knowing how much money you could pull out of the investment over time and the cost to access that equity if you choose to do so.

Trademarks: The World's Greatest Real Estate Deal Analysis Spreadsheet™, Cash Flow from Depreciation™, True Cash Flow, True Net Equity™, and Nomad™ are trademarks of James Orr and/or Real Estate Financial Planner LLC. All rights reserved.

94 Ways to Improve Cash Flow on Rental Properties

You might find yourself in a real estate market where:

- Property prices are high—possibly even soaring,
- Mortgage interest rates are elevated—maybe significantly so,
- Yet rents, despite any increases, haven't risen enough to offset these higher prices and rates.

Instead of the steady stream of cash flow you anticipated, you may be seeing just a trickle.

As a real estate broker, I developed the *Lowest Monthly Payment Guarantee*™ for my clients. This comprehensive checklist—backed by a *cash-in-your-pocket guarantee*—promised to uncover every possible way to reduce and minimize their monthly payments when purchasing a property.

For my real estate investor clients, I went a step further and created the *Maximum Cash Flow Guarantee*™. This second checklist—also backed by a *cash-in-your-pocket guarantee*—was designed to help them identify every possible way to increase and maximize the income generated from their rental properties.

Simply put, cash flow is the difference between income and expenses.

By maximizing income and minimizing expenses on a rental property, you can significantly boost your cash flow.

Below, you'll find an abridged version of these two checklists—combined into one—designed to help you maximize cash flow on your rental properties.

For your convenience, I've organized the strategies into seven distinct stages of the real estate investing process.

7 Distinct Real Estate Investing Stages for Improving Cash Flow

The real estate investing process can be broken down into seven distinct stages, each offering unique opportunities to improve cash flow:

1. **Searching for Properties** - Strategies to enhance cash flow while you're searching for a property to buy.

2. **Financing the Property** - Tactics to maximize cash flow when securing financing for the property you're purchasing.
3. **Improving the Real Estate Investing Strategy** - Different real estate investing strategies produce varying levels of cash flow. Here, you'll find strategies tailored to the specific investing approach you choose once you've acquired the property.
4. **Improving the Property** - Cash flow enhancement strategies based on making physical improvements to the property itself.
5. **Marketing the Property for Rent** - Techniques to boost cash flow during the process of marketing your property to prospective tenants.
6. **While Owning the Property** - Strategies you can implement at any time during ownership to optimize cash flow.
7. **While Renting the Property** - Methods to improve cash flow while actively renting out the property.

While applying strategies from each stage will maximize your cash flow, you can also focus on the stage you're currently in. Implement what you can now, and revisit these strategies regularly to continuously improve—aim for just a 1% improvement each month.

Searching for Properties

Here are the cash flow improving strategies to implement while searching for a property to buy.

- **Agent Selection** - Choosing the right real estate agent can have a significant impact on your investment's cash flow. Some agents offer lower commissions or commission rebates. This money can appear as improved cash flow in the first year or use the money to buy down your mortgage interest rate and get improved cash flow for the life of the loan.

- **Lock/Float** - When securing financing for a property, interest rates can fluctuate. Locking in an interest rate early can protect you from rising rates during the closing process, while floating allows you to benefit from potential rate drops. This decision can directly influence your cash flow by affecting your monthly mortgage payments. This is especially important when buying properties that have extended under contract periods like when buying new construction.

- **Search for Less Expensive Properties** - Lower-priced properties often come with smaller mortgage payments, which can improve cash flow if you're able to get the same rent as their more expensive alternatives. For every $10,000 less expensive the property, you save approximately $50 per month (when mortgage rates are in the 5% range). Some lower priced prices will have commensurately lower rents. Analyze each deal carefully to ensure that the overall income and expenses align to boost your cash flow.

- **Search for Pretty Properties** - Consider purchasing properties that are already in good condition and don't require significant fix-up costs. By doing so, you can allocate funds that would have been used for repairs to

56

increase your down payment or buy down the interest
rate, both of which can lead to better cash flow.

- **Search for Seller Concessions** - Seller concessions
  are contributions from the seller to help cover your
  closing costs. By negotiating for these concessions, you
  can reduce your out-of-pocket expenses or even use
  them to buy down your mortgage interest rate, both of
  which enhance cash flow. Consider searching for
  properties that are offering seller concessions.
- **Search for Creative Financing** - Creative financing
  can offer more favorable terms than traditional loans,
  directly impacting your cash flow. Here are several types
  of creative financing to consider:

  - **Search for Owner Financing** - Owner financing
    involves the seller acting as the lender, which can
    lead to better terms than a traditional bank loan. This
    can reduce your monthly payments and improve cash
    flow. We define owner financing as when the seller
    does not have a mortgage; if they have a mortgage
    that's wrap financing or buying the property subject
    to their existing mortgage which we will cover next.
  - **Search for Wrap Financing** - In wrap financing,
    you agree to pay the seller a monthly amount that
    "wraps" around their existing mortgage. The seller
    keeps their original mortgage in place and continues
    making payments to their lender. You, in turn, make
    payments to the seller that cover both the existing
    mortgage and any additional amount you've agreed
    upon. This can result in a lower overall interest rate
    compared to obtaining new financing, which can

© 2024 James Orr. All rights reserved.

improve your cash flow. Wrap financing also gives the seller the protection of foreclosure rights if you fail to make payments.

- **Search for Subject To**- In a "subject to" arrangement, you take ownership of the property while the seller's original mortgage stays in place. Instead of wrapping a new loan around the old one, you take over making payments directly to the lender on the seller's existing loan. The loan remains in the seller's name, but you're responsible for the payments. You're not formally accountable to the lender—it's not on your credit report—but you are responsible to the seller as per your agreement. This can be advantageous if the seller's mortgage has a lower interest rate than what's currently available. Like wrap financing, this can significantly reduce your mortgage expenses and boost cash flow. However, "subject to" financing typically doesn't offer the seller the same foreclosure protections as wrap financing does.
- **Search for Assumable Loans** - Some loans can be formally transferred from the seller to the buyer, keeping the original interest rate intact. If the seller's loan has a lower interest rate, assuming the loan can significantly boost your cash flow. Since most loan assumptions are for owner-occupant borrowers this strategy likely only applies to those utilizing an owner-occupant investing strategy like house hacking or Nomad™.
- **Search for Rent-To-Own Properties** - Rent-to-own agreements allow you to lease a property with the

option to purchase it later. These arrangements can offer lower initial payments and more flexible terms, which may improve your cash flow compared to traditional financing.

- o **Search for Agreements for Deed** - Also called bond for deed, contract for deed, or installment land contracts, these arrangements let you pay the seller directly over time. You get the deed after fulfilling the contract. This can lead to lower payments and improved cash flow while you're repaying.
- o **Search for Seller Financing** - Seller financing typically involves the seller offering a loan to cover a portion of the purchase price, often as a second mortgage or "carryback" loan. In this scenario, you would secure the primary mortgage from a traditional lender, and the seller finances the remaining balance. For example, if you purchase a property for $200,000, you might get a $160,000 loan from a bank, with the seller providing a $40,000 loan. This setup can result in more favorable terms, such as lower interest rates or flexible payment schedules, improving your overall cash flow. Unlike owner financing, where the seller finances the entire purchase, seller financing usually complements other financing sources, reducing the need for a larger bank loan.

Once you've found a promising property using the strategies above, the next step is to optimize your financing to further enhance your cash flow. Let's explore the various ways you can improve your cash flow during the financing stage of your real estate investment.

Financing the Property

Here are the cash flow improving strategies to implement while financing the property you're buying.

Before Getting Loan

Here are a few strategies to improve cash flow to use before getting your loan.

- **Lender Selection** - Shop around for lenders to find one that offers better interest rates, lower fees, or more favorable terms. Different lenders have varying costs and requirements, so comparing multiple options on the same day can ensure you get the best deal, improving your overall cash flow.
- **Select by Closing Costs** - Some loans come with higher closing costs than others. By selecting a loan with lower closing costs, especially if you plan to finance these costs, you can reduce the amount you need to borrow, leading to better cash flow due to lower monthly payments.
- **Lock/Float** - Decide whether to lock in your interest rate early to protect against potential rate increases before closing, or to float and take advantage of possible rate decreases. Locking your rate provides security, while floating offers flexibility, both of which can impact your cash flow depending on market conditions.

- **Offer Less** - Negotiating a lower purchase price directly reduces the amount you need to finance, leading to lower monthly mortgage payments. This strategy can also leave more of your resources available for other cash flow improvement tactics.

Pay Upfront Instead of Financing

Here are some strategies for improving cash flow that deal with opting to pay fees upfront instead of financing them.

- **Seller Concessions** - Negotiate for the seller to cover some of your closing costs or to provide credits that can be used to buy down your mortgage interest rate. This is almost certainly required to be done at the time you make your offer and not after your offer is accepted. This reduces your upfront cash outlay and can lower your monthly mortgage payments, thereby improving cash flow.
- **Pay Closing Costs** - Paying your closing costs upfront instead of rolling them into your mortgage can reduce the amount you borrow, lowering your monthly payments and improving cash flow over the life of the loan.
- **Pre-Pay PMI** - If you're required to pay Private Mortgage Insurance (PMI), consider pre-paying it in a lump sum rather than monthly. This reduces your ongoing monthly expenses, leading to better cash flow.
- **Staggered Rate** - Opt for a staggered interest rate loan, where the interest rate is lower in the initial years

and increases over time. This can provide you with better cash flow during the early years of the loan when you may need it most.

- **Buy Down Rate** - Pay upfront to lower your mortgage interest rate for the life of the loan. A lower interest rate means a lower monthly payment, which can significantly improve your cash flow over time. For long-term buy and hold real estate investors—especially if you find yourself in a low mortgage interest rate environment—this can be an amazing strategy.

Change/Improve Borrower(s)

These strategies for improving cash flow relate to changing or improving the borrower on the loan.

- **Credit Score** - Improving your credit score can help you secure a lower interest rate and reduce your PMI rate. Both of these improvements lead to lower monthly payments and better cash flow.
- **Add Borrower** - Adding a co-borrower with a strong credit profile to your loan can help you qualify for a better interest rate and lower PMI, both of which can enhance your cash flow.
- **Remove Borrower** - If one borrower has a weaker credit profile, removing them from the loan might result in a better interest rate. This can lead to lower monthly payments and improved cash flow.
- **Loan Partner** - Partnering with someone who has a strong financial profile can help you secure better loan

terms, including lower interest rates and more favorable conditions, which ultimately enhance your cash flow.

Relationship With Lender

These cash flow improving strategies are based on your relationship with the lender or lending institution.

- **Auto Pay Loan** - Setting up automatic payments can sometimes qualify you for a slight reduction in your interest rate, directly improving your cash flow by lowering your monthly mortgage payment. It may show up also as a penalty to the interest rate if you don't use autopay for the mortgage.
- **Additional Accounts** - Maintaining additional accounts or depositing more funds with your lender might earn you a small interest rate reduction, leading to improved cash flow through lower monthly payments. This is more common with commercial loans and relationship banking.

Change Amortization

These strategies to improve your cash flow deal with changing the amortization schedule of the financing you're getting.

- **Interest Only** - An interest-only loan allows you to pay only the interest for a certain period, which significantly reduces your monthly payments. This can boost your cash flow in the short term, though it comes with long-term risks since the principal remains unpaid. You'll need to have a solid plan to deal with the loan balance when the ballon payment date arrives.

- **Negative Amortization** - A negative amortizing loan allows you to pay less than the interest due, causing the loan balance to increase over time. This lowers your initial payments and improves short-term cash flow but increases your debt over time.
- **Rate from Loan Term** - Shortening the loan term (e.g., switching from a 30-year to a 15-year mortgage) can lower your interest rate. However, this typically increases your monthly payments, so it's more about long-term savings than immediate cash flow improvement.
- **Loan Term** - Extending the loan term (e.g., from 30 to 40 years) reduces the monthly payment amount, which can improve your cash flow. However, this means you'll pay more interest over the life of the loan.

Loan Terms

These cash flow improving strategies deal with the terms (details) of the loan itself.

- **Amount Borrowed** - Putting more money down reduces the amount you need to borrow, leading to lower monthly payments. This can improve your cash flow, though it also means tying up more capital in the property.

64

- **Loan-To-Value** - A lower loan-to-value (LTV) ratio, achieved by making a larger down payment, often results in a better interest rate. This lowers your monthly payments and improves cash flow. Not only can putting more down improve your LTV and give you a better interest rate, but it might also reduce your Private Mortgage Insurance (PMI) payment since that's part of the calculation for determining PMI amounts.
- **Adjustable Rate** - An adjustable-rate mortgage (ARM) typically starts with a lower interest rate than a fixed-rate mortgage. This can enhance your cash flow in the initial years, though the rate—and your payments—can increase later.

Private Mortgage Insurance (PMI)

These strategies to improve cash flow deal primarily with Private Mortgage Insurance (PMI).

What is PMI? The lender would prefer you put at least 20% down to finance a property. With 20% down they feel comfortable enough that if you don't pay as agreed they will be able to foreclose, sell the property and get all their money back after the expenses of foreclosure and sale.

You insist on putting less than 20% down.

They may reluctantly agree, but they may charge you a higher interest rate because it is a riskier loan to them. And, additionally, they may insist that you pay a third-party insurance company a fee that insures them in case you default and they're unable to foreclose and sell the property to recoup their entire investment. This third-party insurance company is Private Mortgage Insurance.

It is insurance you pay for to protect the lender in case you default on the loan.

- **Eliminate PMI** - If you can put down at least 20% of the purchase price, you can avoid PMI altogether, significantly reducing your monthly mortgage expenses and improving your cash flow.
- **Pre-Pay PMI** - Paying PMI in a lump sum upfront instead of monthly can reduce your ongoing costs, leading to better cash flow throughout the loan term.
- **Improve Credit** - Enhancing your credit score can help you secure a lower PMI rate or even eliminate PMI altogether if your LTV ratio improves, both of which contribute to better cash flow.
- **Add Borrowers** - Added a borrower to your loan typically reduces PMI and therefore improves cash flow.

Other Properties

These cash flow improving strategies rely on tapping into other properties you own.

Some of these strategies deal with making sure your cash flow is optimized for your entire portfolio (including these other properties) and not specifically to a new property you're buying.

- **Cash Out Refi to Buy/Refi** - Consider doing a cash-out refinance on another property to use the proceeds for purchasing or refinancing your current property. This can result in better overall financing terms and improved cash flow.
- **Cash Out Refi for Larger Down Payment** - If putting more down on your current property will secure a better interest rate or eliminate PMI, consider using funds from a cash-out refinance on another property. This can lower your monthly payments and improve cash flow.
- **Rate and Term Before Acquisition** - Before purchasing a new property, consider refinancing your existing properties to better terms. As you own more properties the complexity of refinancing increases significantly. Consider this a reminder to consider this before each new purchase and to make any changes to other properties now before you add a new property that further limits what you can do. This can also improve the overall cash flow on your portfolio and might also allow you to qualify for better financing on the new purchase.

Non-Traditional Financing

These are some non-traditional financing strategies for improving cash flow you might want to consider.

- **Pay Cash** - If you have sufficient funds, paying cash for a property eliminates the need for financing altogether, which maximizes cash flow by removing monthly mortgage payments.

- **Private Financing** - Secure a loan from family or friends (private lenders) who might offer more favorable terms than traditional banks. This can lead to lower monthly payments and improved cash flow.
- **Creative Financing** - Explore options like owner financing, wrap financing, agreement for deed, lease-options, or subject to, where the seller might offer better terms than traditional lenders. These strategies can lower your mortgage payments and enhance cash flow.
- **Assumable Loan** - If the seller's existing loan has a lower interest rate than current market rates, assuming their loan can be a great way to secure better financing terms, leading to improved cash flow. This is more likely for owner-occupant loans, so this is probably limited to owner-occupant investing strategies like house hacking or Nomad™.

While optimizing your financing is crucial for improving cash flow, it's equally important to consider how your chosen real estate investing strategy can impact your returns. Let's now explore various strategies that can enhance your cash flow by refining your overall investment approach.

Improving the Real Estate Investing Strategy

Here are the cash flow improving strategies based on improving the real estate investing strategy you're opting to utilize.

- **Term** - Adjusting the duration of your lease can significantly impact your cash flow. Shorter-term rentals, such as daily, weekly, or monthly leases, often command higher rents compared to yearly leases. However, shorter terms can also lead to increased expenses, including higher vacancy rates, more frequent marketing, and potentially higher management and maintenance costs. Offering different terms, such as furnished vs. unfurnished rentals, can also cater to various market segments, like vacation rentals or boarding houses, providing opportunities to maximize income.

- **Lease-Option** - Lease-option strategies, including variations like rent-to-own (like lease-purchases and lease-options), can dramatically improve cash flow, particularly in markets where buying is significantly more expensive than renting. These arrangements typically involve collecting a non-refundable purchase deposit/option fee, which can—mathematically—appear to add hundreds of dollars per month to your cash flow. Additionally, tenants in lease-option agreements often treat the property with more care, reducing maintenance, vacancy, and management costs. This strategy is a form of our *Deal Alchemy*™, where you trade future appreciation returns for immediate cash flow.

- **Niche** - Specializing in a specific rental market can allow you to charge premium rents by catering to unique needs. For example, you might focus on corporate rentals, traveling nurses, or student housing. By understanding and addressing the specific requirements of your niche audience, such as providing furnished units for corporate rentals or flexible leases for students, you can add value that justifies higher rental rates. The key is to determine what additional services or amenities you can offer that will attract your target market and what premium you can reasonably charge for those services.

The following cash flow improving strategies are really just variations of house hacking where you're renting out part of the property you're living in for income and to improve cash flow. However, you could utilize these strategies even when you're not living in the property.

- **Roommates** - Renting out individual bedrooms in a single-family home, or additional units in a duplex, triplex, or fourplex, can significantly increase your cash flow. This is a common house hacking strategy where you live in one part of the property and rent out the rest. For example, you might rent out spare bedrooms in your own home or lease the other units in a multi-family property. This approach allows you to maximize the rental income from a single property by utilizing every available space.

- **Rent by Bed/Bedroom** - Some properties, particularly those near colleges or universities, may lend themselves well to renting by the bedroom or even by the bed. This strategy works particularly well with student housing, where multiple tenants share a single property. By renting out each bedroom or bed individually, you can often achieve a higher overall rent compared to leasing the entire property to a single tenant.
- **Rent by Parts** - Renting out different parts of a property, such as non-conforming units in a duplex, triplex, or fourplex, can be a lucrative strategy. It's essential to check local occupancy laws to ensure compliance. This strategy can also include more unconventional setups, such as renting out RV parking spaces, tiny homes, garages, or storage units on the property. These spaces don't have to be residential; they can be rented for commercial or recreational purposes, such as storage or use of shared community amenities like a pool or recreational center.

While optimizing your real estate investing strategy can significantly boost cash flow, another powerful approach is to enhance the property itself. By making strategic improvements and modifications to your rental property, you can potentially increase its value and appeal, leading to higher rental income and improved cash flow. Let's explore some effective strategies for improving cash flow through property enhancements.

Improving the Property

Here are the cash flow improving strategies based on making improvements to the property.

- **Subdivide** - Consider subdividing your property into multiple units to increase rental income. For example, you could rent the upstairs and downstairs separately, offering tenants more privacy while still sharing common areas like heating, cooling, mail, laundry, and possibly even the kitchen or living areas. This isn't the same as converting the property into a formal duplex or triplex; instead, it's more about creating a roommate-like situation with more separation. This setup allows you to comply with local roommate laws and zoning requirements while potentially charging higher rents, as tenants may feel like they have their own space.
- **Upgrade Property** - Enhancing your property's curb appeal and overall condition can justify charging higher rents. Improvements could include landscaping, painting, adding or improving shutters, lawn care, updating the mailbox, property address numbers, or exterior lighting. These upgrades can attract higher-paying tenants and increase the property's value. This approach is also common in value-add strategies or the BRRRR (Buy, Rehab, Rent, Refinance, Repeat) method, where the goal is to improve the property to increase its rent and overall profitability.
- **Solar** - Installing solar panels and including the cost of electricity in the base rent can make your property more attractive to tenants who value energy efficiency,

potentially allowing you to charge higher rents. However, you should be cautious about the legal implications of charging for utilities, as this can sometimes enter a gray area. It's advisable to consult with a local attorney to ensure compliance with utility billing regulations.

- **Furnished Rental** - Offering a furnished rental can significantly increase the rent you can charge, especially if you shift your strategy to short-term or medium-term rentals, such as vacation rentals, student rentals, or corporate housing. Furnished rentals appeal to tenants looking for convenience and are often willing to pay a premium for a move-in ready home.

- **Convert Property** - Converting a single-family property into a duplex, triplex, or fourplex can increase your rental income by creating multiple rental units within the same property. This approach is especially effective if the property is already somewhat set up for such a conversion. However, it may be cost-prohibitive or even impossible if significant structural changes are required or if zoning laws restrict such conversions. Always check with your city and county regarding zoning and licensing requirements before starting any conversion work, as this can also affect the types of loans you can secure and their terms, including the loan-to-value ratio.

- **Improvement Rent** - Charging extra rent for specific property improvements can help offset the cost of upgrades while increasing your overall rental income. For example, you might charge a tenant more for installing new carpet or a fence. While you may not be able to recoup the full cost of the improvement from a single tenant, some upgrades, like a fence, can justify higher rents with future tenants as well, allowing you to gradually recover your investment and potentially earn a return. This strategy is particularly useful for items with a long lifespan, where the cost can be spread out over multiple tenancies.

While property improvements can significantly boost your rental income, the way you market your property can be equally important for maximizing cash flow. By implementing effective marketing strategies, you can attract high-quality tenants, reduce vacancy periods, and potentially command higher rents. Let's explore some key strategies for improving cash flow through smart marketing techniques.

Marketing the Property for Rent

Here are the cash flow improving strategies to implement while you're marketing your property for rent.

- **Optimize Marketing** - Effective marketing starts with high-quality materials. Ensure that you have professional-grade photos, a 3D tour, and a video to showcase your property. These elements can significantly enhance the appeal of your listing, attracting more potential tenants. Additionally, use online marketing as well as flyers and signs strategically around the neighborhood to increase visibility. Well-designed marketing materials make your property stand out and convey a sense of professionalism that can justify higher rent and reduce vacancy periods.

- **Maximize Exposure** - To attract the right tenants, it's crucial to advertise your property across all available platforms where tenants might be searching. This includes online rental websites, social media, and community bulletin boards. Physical advertising, such as yard signs and directional signs leading to the property, can also capture the attention of local renters. By maximizing exposure, you increase the chances of filling vacancies quickly and with quality tenants.

- **Sales Skills** - Mastering sales skills is essential for renting your property at the highest possible rate and minimizing vacancy. This includes both phone skills for initial inquiries and in-person salesmanship during property tours. Being persuasive and knowledgeable helps you connect with potential tenants, address their concerns, and highlight the property's best features, ultimately leading to faster lease agreements and better tenant retention.

- **Optimize Showings** - Preparing your property for showings is a key step in securing a lease. Ensure the property is well-lit, smells pleasant, and is clean, neat, and in good repair. First impressions matter, and a well-presented property can make the difference between a potential tenant choosing your property over another. Additionally, create a sense of scarcity by scheduling back-to-back showings and mentioning this when booking appointments. This strategy can create urgency and increase interest among prospective tenants.

While effective marketing strategies can help attract tenants and maximize rental income, it's equally important to focus on optimizing your property's financial performance during ownership. Let's explore various strategies you can implement to improve cash flow throughout your tenure as a property owner.

While Owning the Property

Here are the cash flow improving strategies to implement while you own the property.

Refi/Pay Off Loan

Managing your mortgage can be one of the most effective ways to improve cash flow and overall property profitability.

- **Refi to Extend Term** - If your loan is old enough, consider refinancing to extend the loan term. This can lower your monthly payments and—if interest rates have dropped and/or your loan-to-value has improved—potentially secure a better interest rate, improving your cash flow.
- **Refi to Improve Rate** - If interest rates have dropped since you first took out your mortgage, refinancing to a lower rate can reduce your monthly payments and save you money over the life of the loan.
- **Payoff Loan** - If you have the financial means, paying off your loan in its entirety can eliminate your mortgage payments, drastically improving your monthly cash flow and reducing financial stress.

Taxes

Property taxes are a significant expense for any property owner, and managing them effectively can save you money.

- **Correct Assessor** - Ensure that the county assessor has accurate information about your property's condition and characteristics. Correcting any inaccuracies can prevent overvaluation and keep your taxes in check.
- **Contest Tax Increases** - If your property taxes increase, consider contesting the increase. Successful challenges can lead to reduced tax bills and improved cash flow.
- **Vote** - Participate in local elections and vote on measures that affect property taxes. Being informed and voting appropriately can help control future tax increases.

Insurance

Insurance is essential for protecting your investment, but it's also an area where you can manage costs.

- **Shop Insurance Rates** - Regularly compare insurance rates from different providers to ensure you're getting the best deal. Competitive rates can lower your insurance costs without sacrificing coverage.
- **Insurance Coverage** - Review your property insurance policy to make sure you have the right level of coverage. Avoid overpaying for unnecessary coverage or underinsuring your property. It is not just about

minimizing this cost while sacrificing coverage; you must make sure you minimize cost while keeping a desirable level of coverage. Sacrificing coverage is short-sighted and might significantly hurt cash flow if you ever have a claim that is you opted not to cover.

- **Insured** - Adjust your insurance policy by adding or removing people as needed to optimize your rates. This can lead to lower premiums.
- **Insurance Deductible** - Consider raising your deductible to lower your insurance premium. Taking on more risk personally can reduce your monthly insurance costs. See comments about sacrificing coverage being short-sighted above.
- **Remove PMI** - Totally different type of insurance, but if your property's equity has increased sufficiently, you may be able to remove Private Mortgage Insurance (PMI). This can significantly reduce your monthly mortgage payment.

Making Payments

How you manage your payments can also impact your overall costs.

- **Discount for Autopay** - Sign up for autopay on utilities and other bills to avoid per-bill fees. Many service providers offer small discounts or waive fees for customers who enroll in autopay.
- **Discount for Early Payments** - Some service providers, such as HOA or insurance companies, offer

78

discounts for early payments. Paying these bills in advance can reduce your overall expenses.

Management

Whether you manage your property yourself or hire a professional, effective management is key to maintaining profitability.

- **Self-Manage** - If you choose to manage the property yourself, ensure you stay up to date with the latest laws, best practices, and compliance issues. Self-management can save on property management fees, but it often requires a significant time investment.
- **Professional Property Manager** - Shop around for a high-quality property manager who offers reasonable fees. A good property manager can maximize your rental income and minimize headaches.
- **Manage the Manager** - Even with a professional property manager, it's important to regularly review management statements for accuracy. Mistakes can happen, and catching them early can save you money.
- **Insist on Best Practices** - Ensure your property manager follows best practices, such as marketing your property early and raising rents with each lease renewal. This proactive approach can help maximize your rental income.

© 2024 James Orr. All rights reserved.

Maintenance

Regular maintenance is crucial for keeping your property in good condition and minimizing vacancies.

- **Maintain Property** - Regularly maintaining your property can reduce the time it spends vacant between tenants. A well-maintained property attracts tenants quickly and reduces downtime.
- **Quality Materials** - Using quality materials for maintenance and repairs may have a higher upfront cost, but it can lower the overall cost of maintenance over time by reducing the frequency of repairs and replacements.

Depreciation

Depreciation can provide significant tax benefits, and managing it strategically can enhance your investment returns.

- **Accelerate Depreciation** - Consider accelerating depreciation on your property to maximize tax benefits in the short term. This strategy can improve your cash flow by reducing your taxable income, but it should be used with careful planning to avoid potential future tax liabilities. This can be one of the larger improvements to your cash flow.

While the strategies for improving cash flow during property ownership are crucial, it's equally important to optimize your rental income while renting it. Let's explore various techniques you can implement to enhance your cash flow during the rental phase of your investment.

While Renting the Property

Here are the cash flow improving strategies to implement while you're renting the property.

Add Services

Offering additional services can increase rental income and enhance tenant satisfaction.

- **Additional Services** - Consider offering additional services such as high-speed internet, cable, or utilities for an extra fee. Tenants often value the convenience of bundled services, making this an effective way to boost your rental income. However, be sure to check local laws, as this practice may not be permitted in some areas.
- **DFY Services** - Offer done-for-you (DFY) services such as lawn care, snow removal, or house cleaning. These services can be billed as extras, appealing to tenants who prefer convenience and are willing to pay for it.

Charge Appropriately

Setting appropriate charges can maximize your rental income while offering flexibility to tenants.

- **Bill Back** - Implement bill-back strategies for utilities or HOA services, such as charging tenants for non-potable water or other shared resources. This helps to ensure that tenants are covering their fair share of costs, improving your net income.
- **Tier Rent by Credit Score** - Adjust rent based on the tenant's credit score, with higher rent for those with lower scores. This can also apply to security deposits, where tenants with better credit pay less upfront. Check with your attorney before implementing this strategy.
- **Pet Rent** - Charge additional rent for tenants with pets. Pet rent can help cover potential wear and tear caused by pets and increase your overall rental income.

Convenience Billing

Convenience billing options can make it easier for tenants to pay rent while potentially increasing your revenue.

- **Billing Frequency** - Offer more frequent billing options, such as weekly or biweekly payments, instead of the traditional monthly schedule. This can be attractive to tenants who prefer smaller, more manageable payments but can also produce more cash flow over the same period.
- **Autopay** - Here are conflicting ideas where both options may ultimately improve cash flow. Encourage tenants to enroll in autopay by offering a discount or, conversely, charge a fee for those who do not use autopay. Autopay

can reduce late payments and ensure consistent cash flow.

- **Discount On-Time Payment** - Provide a discount for tenants who pay their rent on time or early, incentivizing prompt payments and reducing the need for late payment penalties.
- **Term** - Adjust the term of rental agreements to fit different rental strategies. Consider offering daily, weekly, or short-term/vacation rentals, which can often command higher rents than traditional monthly leases.

Timing

Optimizing the timing of lease agreements and renewals can minimize vacancies and maximize rental income.

- **Notice** - Require a 60-90 day notice from tenants if they intend not to renew their lease. This provides you with ample time to market the property and secure a new tenant, reducing vacancy periods.
- **Start Early/Test Rent** - Begin marketing the property early, even before the current tenant moves out, and start with a higher rent to test the market. This strategy allows you to adjust pricing based on demand and secure the best possible rental rate.
- **Renew Peak Season** - Align lease renewal dates to end during peak rental seasons, such as spring or summer, when demand is higher. This increases the likelihood of filling the property quickly and possibly at a higher rent.

Miscellaneous

Implementing additional requirements can protect your property and reduce potential liabilities.

- **Renter's Insurance** - Require tenants to carry renter's insurance. This protects both you and the tenant in case of damage to the property or loss of personal belongings, reducing potential conflicts and liabilities.

Conclusion

This guide has explored 94 ways to improve cash flow on rental properties across seven distinct stages of your real estate investing process.

Each stage presents unique opportunities to boost your investment's financial performance, and the cumulative effect of applying these strategies can significantly increase your property's profitability.

By focusing on cash flow improvement at every stage, you can:

- Build a more resilient and profitable real estate portfolio
- Enhance property values—especially for properties where value is driven by the income they generate, such as commercial properties
- Strengthen your ability to secure favorable financing by improving loan-to-value (LTV) and debt service coverage ratios
- Optimize tax benefits

84

- Accelerate savings for larger down payments and quickly replenish reserves
- Increase tenant satisfaction by enhancing the tenant experience, improving retention rates, and reducing turnover costs

Remember, even small adjustments across multiple areas can compound into substantial gains in your overall returns and financial stability.

Make it a habit to regularly review and implement these strategies, tailoring them to fit your specific properties and market conditions.

With consistent effort and strategic application, you can transform your rental properties into powerful, cash-generating assets that support your long-term financial goals.

Introduction to Monte Carlo Analysis of Rental Properties

There's a problem with how we've been modeling our investments so far. It is not unique to us. Almost everyone does it wrong.

But, we're going to fix it now.

The issue is the assumptions we've been using and how the real world works.

The World's Greatest Real Estate Deal Analysis Spreadsheet™

For the analysis we've been doing with *The World's Greatest Real Estate Deal Analysis Spreadsheet*™ (TWGREDAS)—and any other real estate deal analysis spreadsheet—we've used static assumptions.

We might assume that property values are going up by 3% per year. Well, that's not truly a correct representation of reality.

Heck, with the overrides tab in TWGREDAS we may have said, they go up by 3% for the first 3 years and then only 2% thereafter. Better, but still not reality.

The truth is: we really don't know how much property values will go up as we hold the property. They could go up by 3%. They could go down by 3%. They could go up then down or down then up. Could be more or less than 3%. Might be 3.1% or 2.9%. Might be up or down 6% or 10%.

If we look back at history (and we do when we consider the risks of investing in real estate), we can see what property appreciation has done over the last 100 years.

Risk Matrix: Appreciation

Likelihood	0 Increase	1 Small Decline	2 Medium Decline	3 Large Decline	4 Catastrophic
	Severity				
1	>10% Increase 7.7%			10-15% Decline 6.0%	>15% Decline 0.0%
2	5-10% Increase 15.0%		5-10% Decline 12.8%		
3	0-5% Increase 25.6%	0-5% Decline 34.6%			

So, to correctly model how our investment might perform, we should not use a static 3% per year—or whatever static number you believe to be true—for property appreciation.

Our crystal balls are broken. We can't accurately predict—exactly—what appreciation will be for our properties.

We can guess. Based on what has happened in the past they will average about 3% per year.

But they may:

- Increase in value by more than 10% for the year about 7.7% of the time
- Increase between 5% and 10% for the year about 15% of the time
- Increase between 0% and 5% for the year about 25.6% of the time
- Go down in value between 0% and 5% for the year about 34.6% of the time

- Go down in value between 5% and 10% for the year about 12.8% of the time
- Go down in value between 10% and 15% for the year about 6% of the time

These are based on what has happened over the last 100 years. Could the future be different? Absolutely.

But it is much more accurate than just assuming that they will be going up in value by 3% per year every year.

Not Just Property Appreciation

As you probably guessed, this isn't just an issue with property appreciation. It applies to other assumptions we have as well.

Here's a list of some of the more significant ones:

- **Property Appreciation Rate** - This is the one we've been talking about already. It is how much properties go up or down in value.
- **Rent Appreciation Rate** - This is how much rents increase or decrease with each lease renewal.
- **Inflation Rate** - Inflation reflects the overall increase in prices and the decrease in purchasing power over time. It impacts everything from the cost of goods and services to the value of money itself. In the context of your portfolio, inflation affects how much your money will be worth in the future, influencing the real returns on your investments. For instance, even if your rental

income and property values rise, high inflation could erode those gains in terms of actual purchasing power. A million dollars today isn't the same as a million dollars 50 years ago and it won't be the same as a million dollars 50 years from now.

- **Mortgage Interest Rates - Mortgage Interest Rates** - Mortgage rates fluctuate over time. The rate you secure for your current property purchase or refinance won't necessarily be the same for properties you buy in one, five, or more years from now.
- **Stock Market Rate of Return** - This is how much you're earning on money you have invested in the stock market. This also applies to other investments you might have like savings accounts, bonds, CDs, cryptocurrencies, etc.

If you really want to go to freaky town, you could also model this with changing tax rates, insurance rates, maintenance and capital expenses on the property.

Does This Even Matter?

Does this even matter and why should I care?

Let's start with a simple example of someone who invests in stocks. They don't even buy a home to live in; they rent instead.

They invest approximately 10% of their income in the stock market earning 8% per year.

Using static assumptions, we could calculate that they would be financially independent (FI) after about 53.25 years.

See **Figure 1** at the end of the chapter. We moved the charts to the end of the chapter so we could show you larger, readable versions of the charts.

But what if we used a reasonable range of values for the return from the stock market instead of always 8% every year?

We could use a range of values that better approximates what the stock markets has done historically—still averaging about 8% for this selection of stocks.

Instead of seeing a smooth line showing their journey toward financial independence as shown in **Figure 2** at the end of the chapter.

We'd instead see a less smooth line representing how the stock market returns change each month like **Figure 3**.

And, if we ran it 10 times, you'd see that when they actually achieve financial independence (when the line crosses the horizontal dotted line) is a little different each time. See **Figure 4**.

If the stock market performs well, they're financially independent earlier. If the stock market does not perform as well, they end up being financially independent later.

If we ran this 1,000 times and summarized the results, we can see the range of when they're financially independent. See **Figure 5**.

Monte Carlo Modeling

This type of analysis is called Monte Carlo modeling.

Monte Carlo modeling is a statistical technique used to simulate multiple potential outcomes for an investment or financial scenario.

It works by:

- Running hundreds or thousands of simulations with varying input parameters
- Analyzing the range and probability of different outcomes
- Providing a more nuanced understanding of potential risks and returns

For real estate investing, Monte Carlo analysis involves varying input factors such as property appreciation rates, rent increases, mortgage interest rates, inflation, and market returns. This approach allows you to better assess the likelihood of achieving your financial goals and understand the potential risks associated with your investment strategies.

I like to call it *Alternate Universe Modeling*™ because we're consider how your investments might perform if you were living in alternate universes with different futures.

Back to our example with someone just investing in stocks.

In **Figure 5** at the end of the chapter:

- The light blue band shows the full range of results from the very worst to the very best.
- The darker blue band in the middle shows you the middle 50% of all runs. Half of the time the results are this darker band.
- The dark link at the very center shows you the median value. Half the values are higher than this. Half the values are lower than this.

If we look at the median line we can see that half the time they're financially independent around 58 years. Half the time it is after 58 years.

It could have been as early as year 48. And, it could take longer than 60 years—when we stopped modeling for this example. In fact, only about 85% of the 1,000 runs we ran were financially independent 60 years from when they started.

We can summarize this is a different chart and show what percentage of the 1,000 runs were financially independent in each month. That's **Figure 6**.

By using a range of values for things like the stock market rate of return, we get a much more nuanced understanding of what is likely to happen.

What If They Became Homeowners Instead of Renting?

Our last example they were renting a property to live in and investing in stocks.

What if they bought on owner-occupant property with 5% down to live in and invested in stocks?

If we used static assumptions they would be financially independent about 15 and half years faster as shown in **Figure 7** at the end of the chapter.

Part of what gets them to financial independence faster is that they end up paying off their owner-occupant property 30 years after they buy it. Without a mortgage payment the threshold for them being financially independent is a little lower.

There's a little more to this story, but I don't want to go off into the weeds here. The punchline is they achieve financial independence faster with static assumptions as you can see in **Figure 8**.

Let's vary the property appreciation rate, mortgage interest rate, inflation rate, and stock market rate of return. If we were discussing rentals, we'd vary the rent appreciation rate as well but in this case they're not buying any rentals; we'll get to that shortly.

With variable property appreciation rates, mortgage interest rates until they lock in a 30-year fixed rate financing loan, inflation rate and stock market rate of return it looks like **Figure 9**.

They're financially independent as early as 33.75 years from when they start. In 99.5% of the 1,000 runs they're financially independent by the time we stop modeling at 60 years.

How does this compare to them just investing in stocks? Let's show both on one chart in **Figure 10**.

Buying an owner-occupant property seems to make a pretty big difference.

If we just look at what percentage of the 1,000 runs they achieve financial independence, you can see that buying the owner-occupant property is more probable (higher percentage of the runs achieve it) and they're financially independent earlier (it happens more to the left on the chart). See **Figure 11**.

Buying Rental Properties with 20% Down Payments

Let's assume, for now, that they don't buy an owner-occupant property with 5% down. Instead, they decide to buy 20% down rental properties as their primary investing strategy.

Any additional money beyond what they need for the rentals is still investing in stocks, but whenever they get enough for a 20% down payment they buy a rental property with very modest cash flow.

They're willing to buy up to ten 20% down payment rentals.

If we have **static assumptions** for property appreciation, rent appreciation, inflation, mortgage interest rates and the stock market rate of return, they might be financially independent after 31 years.

With static assumptions, that's about 18.67 years faster than just investing in stocks and about 3 years faster than buying an owner-occupant property and investing stocks as shown in **Figure 12**.

With static assumptions, they achieve financial independence faster. See **Figure 13**.

And, still looking at the chart above, they appear have a lot more income coming then just investing in stocks the longer they hold the rental properties.

In fact, they're earning about twice what they need to be financially independent about 48.5 years in. That means they're earning twice what they need to be financially independent before just investing in stocks as a renter is even earning enough for them to financially independent at all.

Not long after they achieve financial independence just investing in stocks as a renter, they're earning 3 times what they need to be financially independent with their 10 rentals.

96

But, this is about Monte Carlo modeling, so what if we did vary property appreciation rates, rent appreciation rates, inflation, mortgage interest rates and the stock market rate of return?

It is important to realize that because the property prices vary with each run sometimes the properties they're buying can be slightly more or less expensive. On average though, property prices are going up at about 3% per year.

Rent is similar. Rents can go up or down, but overall, rents are increasing by about 3% per year.

Mortgage interest rates started at about 8.5% for a non-owner-occupant loan without paying significant points. But, mortgage interest rates can get better—or worse—over time as they're acquiring properties. That means sometimes properties will cash flow better and sometimes they'll cash flow a little worse.

Let's look at their journey to financial independence buying ten 20% down payment rentals in **Figure 14**.

You can see there are times when the market goes in their favor (both the real estate and stock market) they achieve financial independence early. And, there are times when they still don't quite achieve it through 60 years.

How does it compare to the two previous strategies: renting and investing exclusively in stocks and buying an owner-occupant property and exclusively investing in stocks? See **Figure 15**.

It is getting harder to see what is happening in the chart as we add additional comparisons.

We can make it easier in two different ways. First, we can look at the same chart, but turn off the shaded areas for each strategy.

This would leave just the median—or the middle-most result—where half of them are better and half are worse. That's **Figure 16**.

This chart doesn't show up the range of results (how early or late they achieve FI) but it does show how much more they're likely to earn by buying the rentals by what percent of their financial independence goal they're earning.

By earning a higher percentage of the amount they need to be financially independent, they're able to support a higher standard of living.

In other words, if they needed to be earning $10,000 per month passively to be considered financially independent, but their earning 200% of that—or $20,000 per month—they could live at a much higher standard of living on $20,000 per month than the $10,000 per month that they needed—at a minimum—to be considered financially independent.

The second way to make it easier to see what is happening is looking at the percentage of the 1,000 runs that achieved financial independence like we did previously. That's **Figure 17**.

98

Buying ten 20% down payment rentals sees them achieving financial independence earlier (more left on the chart above) and then has a similar success rate to what they'd see if they bought an owner-occupant and invested in stocks.

Owner-Occupant, Rentals and Stocks

I think you know what's coming next: what if they bought an owner-occupant property with 5% down, then bought up to nine more rental properties, each with 20% down payments and invested the rest in stocks?

With static assumptions that's about 3.5 years faster than just renting and buying ten 20% down payment rentals. See **Figure 18**.

If we do Monte Carlo modeling, it looks like **Figure 19**.

Doing a very busy version of this chart by comparing it to the other strategies so far, it looks like **Figure 20**.

If we just look at the 50th percentile (median) value for the four options as seen in **Figure 21**.

It shows that buying the owner-occupant property and nine 20% down payment rentals appears to be faster and gives them a higher standard of living than even buying ten 20% down payment rentals.

If we look at the percentage of the 1,000 runs for reach strategy that achieved financial independence and when, we can see that buying an owner-occupant property and then nine 20% down rentals is the best performer yet as seen in **Figure 22**.

In the chart above you can see that not only does financial independence tend to happen faster (a little to the left on the chart), it also tends to be more consistent (a higher percentage of the runs achieve FI).

Nomad™ Real Estate Investing Strategy Example

There's so much more we could do with this, but for now I'll wrap it up with a slight curve ball.

Instead of buying an owner-occupant property and then buying nine 20% down payment rentals, let's imagine they Nomad™.

- They buy an owner-occupant property with 5% down payment.
- They live there for *at least* a year. That's a requirement of the lender to get an owner-occupant loan with an owner-occupant down payment and owner-occupant mortgage interest rate.
- Once their year is up AND they've saved up enough for another 5% down payment, they buy another owner-occupant property and move into it.
- They take the previous property they were living in and convert it to a rental property
- They repeat this until they have 9 rentals and the property they're living in

100

Instead of having to save up for 20% down payments, they acquire the same nine rental properties with only 5% down on each by moving into each one as an owner-occupant.

Is this better? Is this more probable for them to be financially independent? Is this faster to financial independence? Does this give a higher standard of living than the other strategies so far? And—we won't cover it here because it is a longer discussion—but is it more or less risky?

It turns out that with static assumptions (not Monte Carlo modeling yet), Nomad™ is 58 months (almost 5 years) faster to financial independence. See **Figure 23**.

If we add variability and do Monte Carlo modeling, we can look at how the Nomad™ strategy performs in **Figure 24**.

Brace yourself for the busy version comparing them all at the same time in **Figure 25**.

And, if we turn off the range of results and just look at the middle most (median) of the 1,000 runs for each strategy, we can see the following in **Figure 26**.

Still a bit busy to see what is going on, but I will point out, in the chart above, the Nomad™ strategy seems to give them the fastest achievement of financial independence and highest standard of living.

Isn't it interesting.

If we look at the percentage of the 1,000 runs that achieve financial independence and by when you can see even better in **Figure 27**.

The Nomad™ strategy achieves financial independence earliest (to the left on the chart above). It also has a higher probability of being financially independent earlier.

Additional Modeling

Now that we know the importance of considering the variability that might occur in the future, this is really just the beginning.

There is a ridiculous amount more to dig into here. We've just barely scratched the surface.

There's a lot more to model.

For example, we could model each strategy you're considering seeing how each strategy performs:

- Buying long-term buy and hold rental properties (short-term rentals, medium-term rentals, student rentals, storage units, assisted living, apartments, etc)
- Buying properties utilizing creative financing (owner financing, wrap financing, loan assumptions, rent-to-owns, agreements for deed, subject-to)
- Variations on the Nomad™ strategy (Nomad™ by Proxy, Nomad™ with House Hacking, Nomad™ to Short-Term Rental, Nomad™ with Lease-Option Exits, *The Ultimate Real Estate Agent Retirement Plan™*)
- House Hacking and related strategies

- Short-Term Rentals and related strategies
- Flipping properties and related strategies
- BRRRR and related strategies
- And much, much more

Or, combining one or more of these strategies at the same time (fix and flipping while acquiring long-term or short-term rentals as an example) or sequentially (fix and flipping for 10 years then switch to buy and hold).

Or, we could test a wide assortment of variations to your strategy:

- More or less reserves (and its impact on both speed and risk)
- More or less down payment size up to buying properties for all cash
- Buying down interest rates or not
- Getting roommates or not (house hacking)
- Selling via lease-options versus with a real estate agent or for sale by owner
- Paying off properties early with extra cash flow versus not
- Doing cash out refinances to buy additional properties faster
- Buying properties and selling them when you could take the proceeds (after all expenses including taxes) and then investing that money in stocks, bonds or something else to be financially independent
- Buying more properties than you need and selling them to pay off properties when it means you'd be financially independent

- And much, much more

Not Just Financial Independence

When we do these models, it is important to consider more than just how fast you're able to get to financial independence—even though that's what we focused on here.

Sometimes it is about your standard of living once you are financially independent. Some strategies might just barely get you to your minimum required income to be financially independent. While others will give you far more each month than you initially stated you needed allowing you to live at a much higher standard of living than you originally required.

Sometimes, it is about measuring, comparing and ultimately minimizing risks. Some strategies are riskier than others. They might get you to financial independence, on average, 1 year faster, but there's a 20 times greater chance you'll run out of money by pursuing that strategy than another one that gets you to financial independence, on average, a year slower.

That all might be worth considering... especially for your own unique situation.

It is important for you to evaluate your own strategy utilizing Monte Carlo modeling to better understand how to achieve financial independence faster, easier, with higher probability of success, with a higher standard of living and with less overall risk.

Or, if you are going to ignore one or more of those things, deliberately and strategically choosing to ignore them with full knowledge of the consequences.

Figure 1

Figure 2

Figure 3

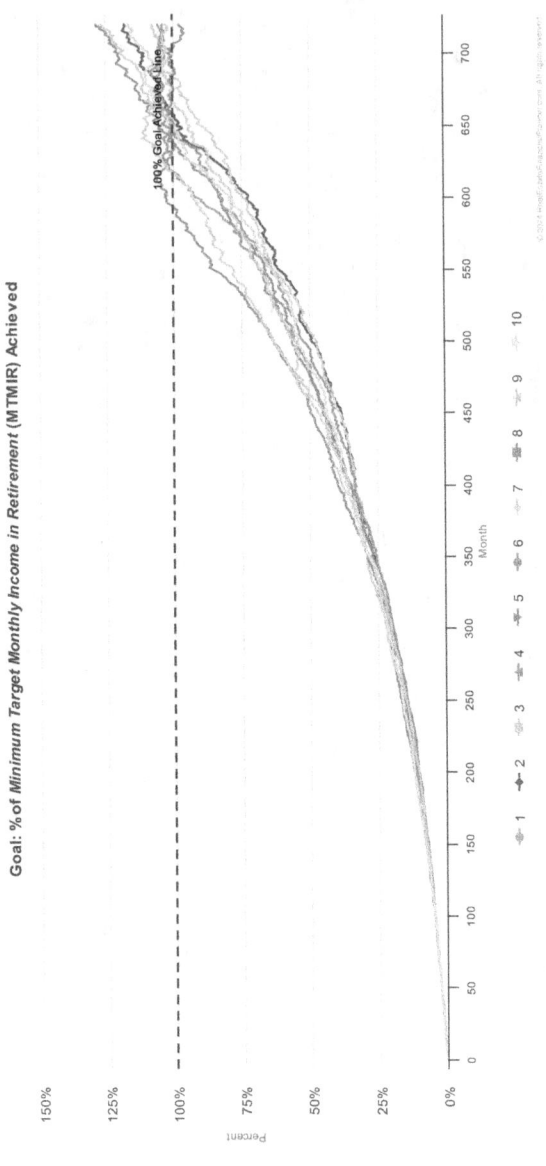

Goal: % of Minimum Target Monthly Income in Retirement (MTMIR) Achieved

Figure 4

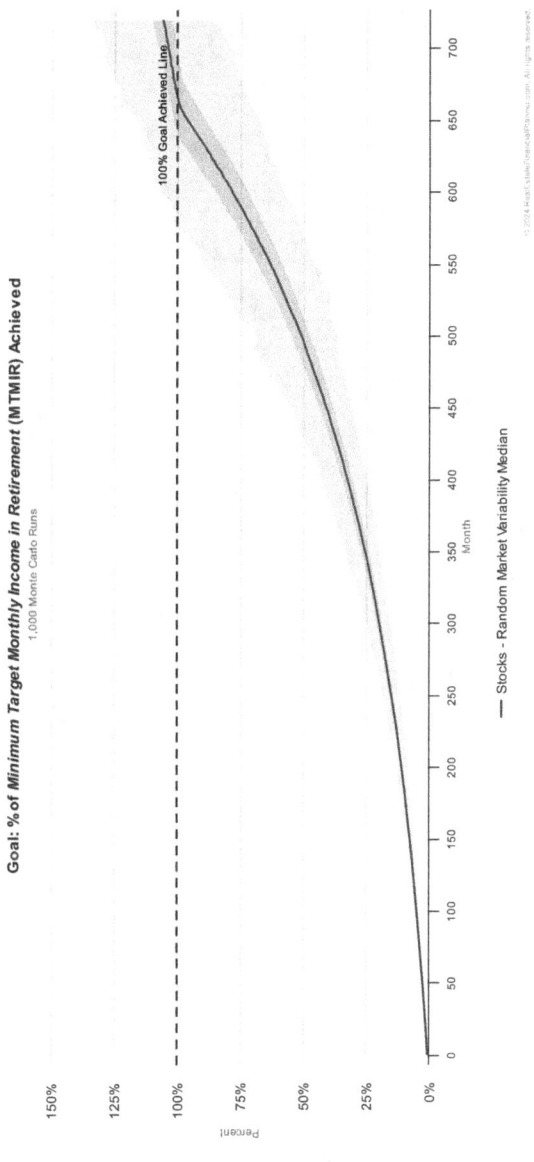

Goal: % of Minimum Target Monthly Income in Retirement (MTMIR) Achieved

1,000 Monte Carlo Runs

100% Goal Achieved Line

— Stocks - Random Market Variability Median

Figure 5

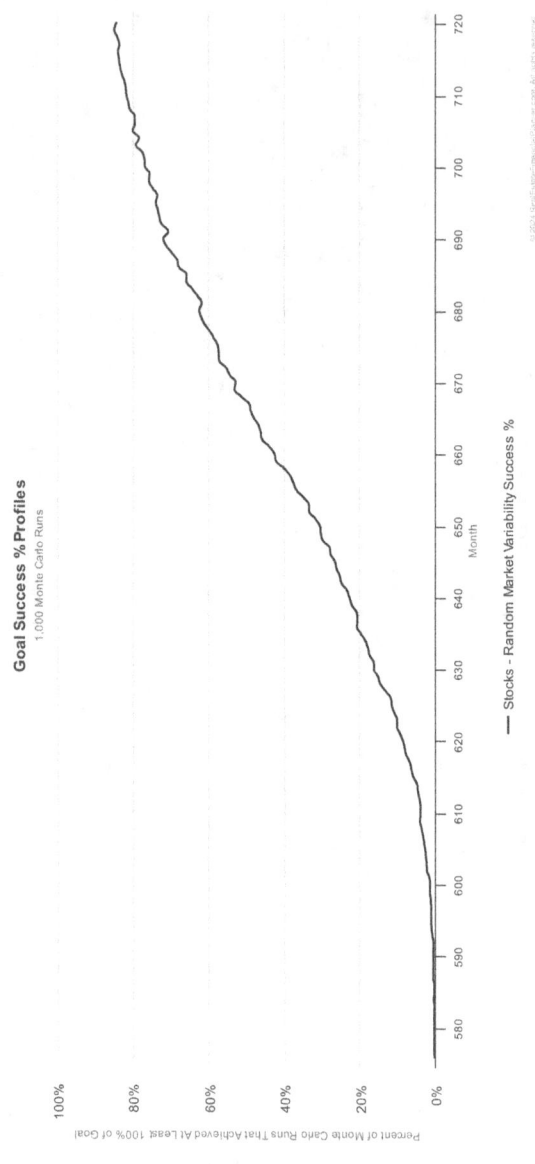

Goal Success % Profiles
1,000 Monte Carlo Runs

Percent of Monte Carlo Runs That Achieved At Least 100% of Goal

Month

— Stocks - Random Market Variability Success %

Figure 6

Figure 7

Figure 8

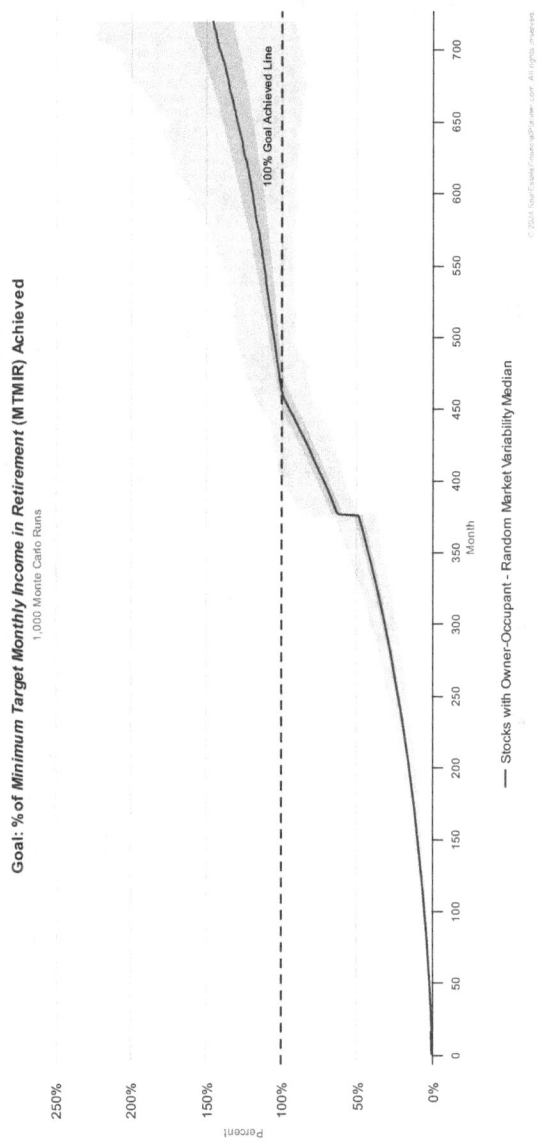

Goal: % of Minimum Target Monthly Income in Retirement (MTMIR) Achieved
1,000 Monte Carlo Runs

— Stocks with Owner-Occupant - Random Market Variability Median

Figure 9

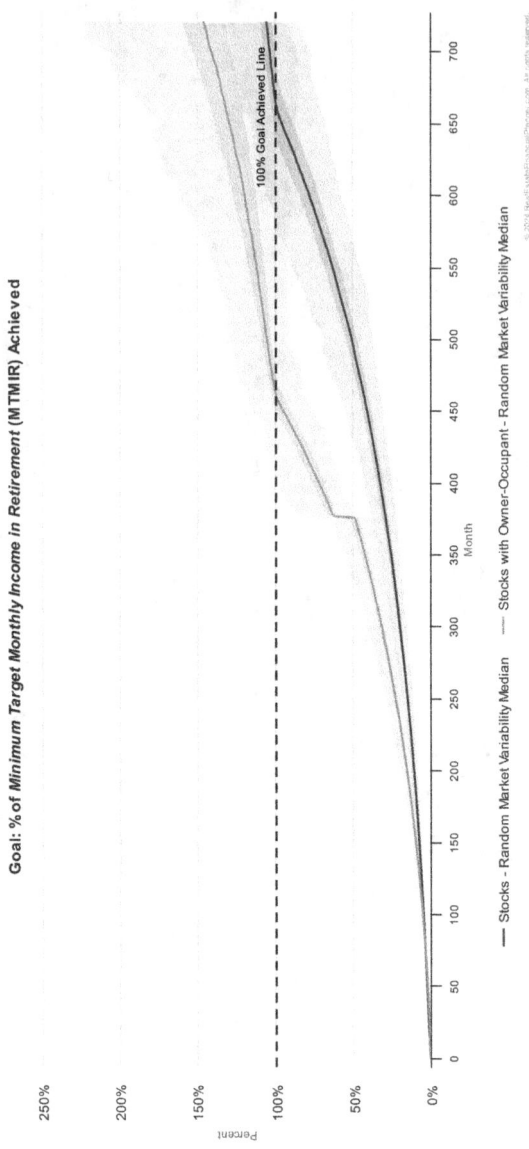

Goal: % of *Minimum Target Monthly Income in Retirement (MTMIR) Achieved*

Figure 10

115

Figure 11

© 2024 James Orr. All rights reserved.

Figure 12

Figure 13

Figure 14

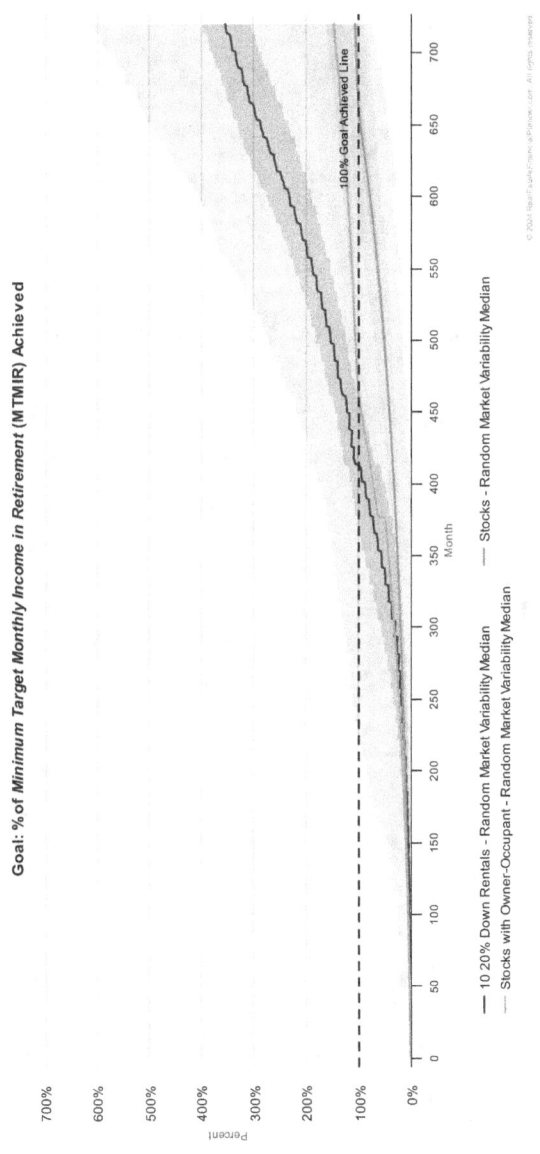

Goal: % of *Minimum Target Monthly Income in Retirement (MTMIR)* Achieved

Figure 15

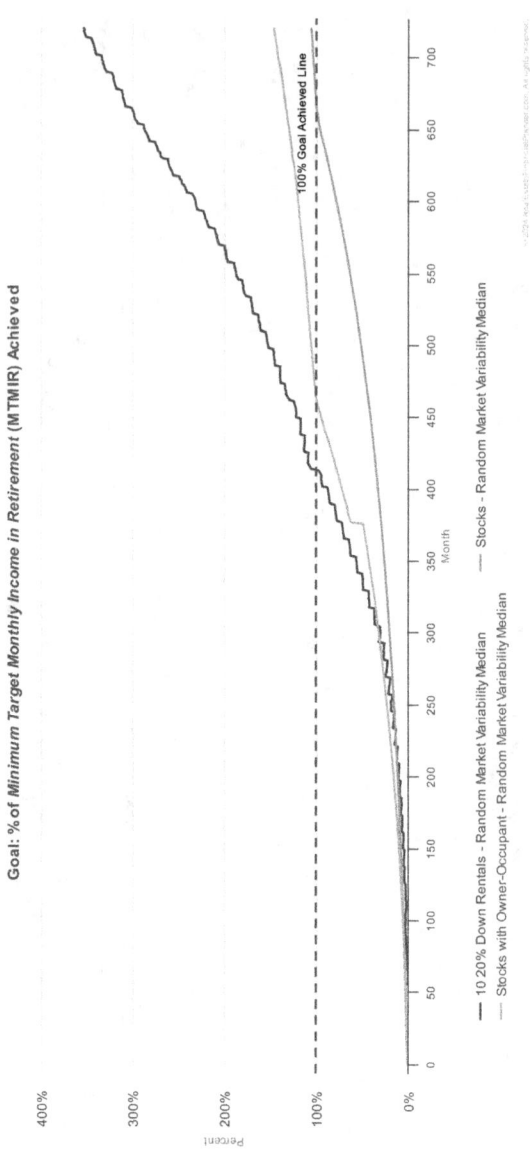

Goal: % of *Minimum Target Monthly Income in Retirement (MTMIR)* Achieved

Figure 16

Figure 17

Figure 18

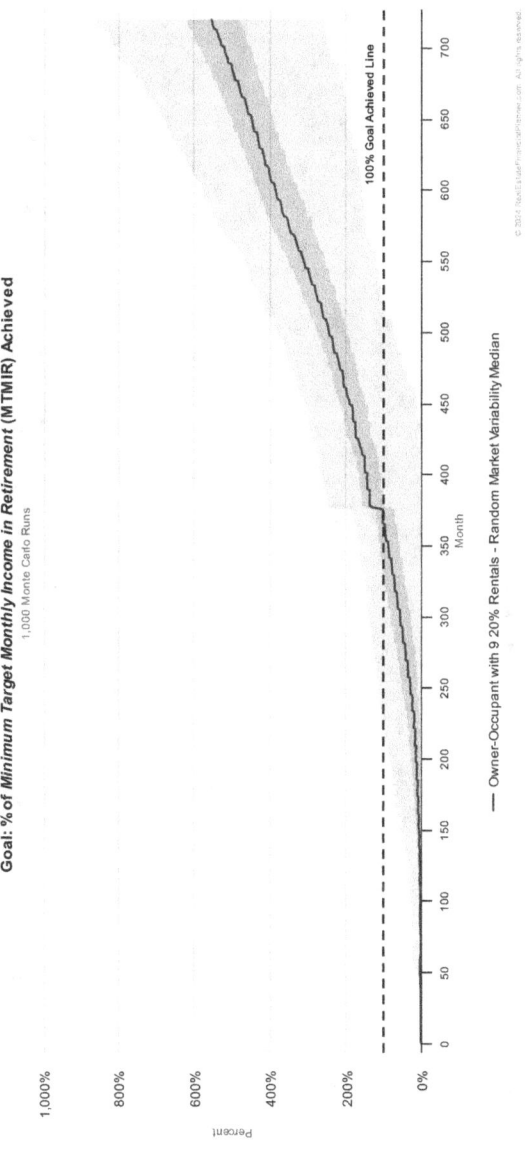

Goal: % of Minimum Target Monthly Income in Retirement (MTMIR) Achieved

1,000 Monte Carlo Runs

100% Goal Achieved Line

— Owner-Occupant with 9 20% Rentals - Random Market Variability Median

Figure 19

Figure 20

Figure 21

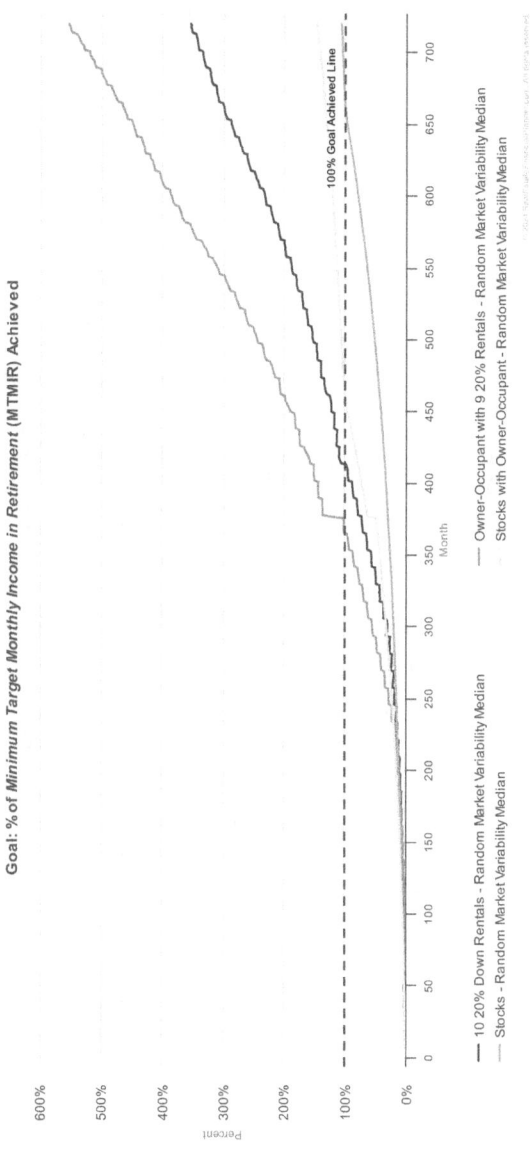

Goal: % of *Minimum Target Monthly Income in Retirement (MTMIR)* Achieved

125

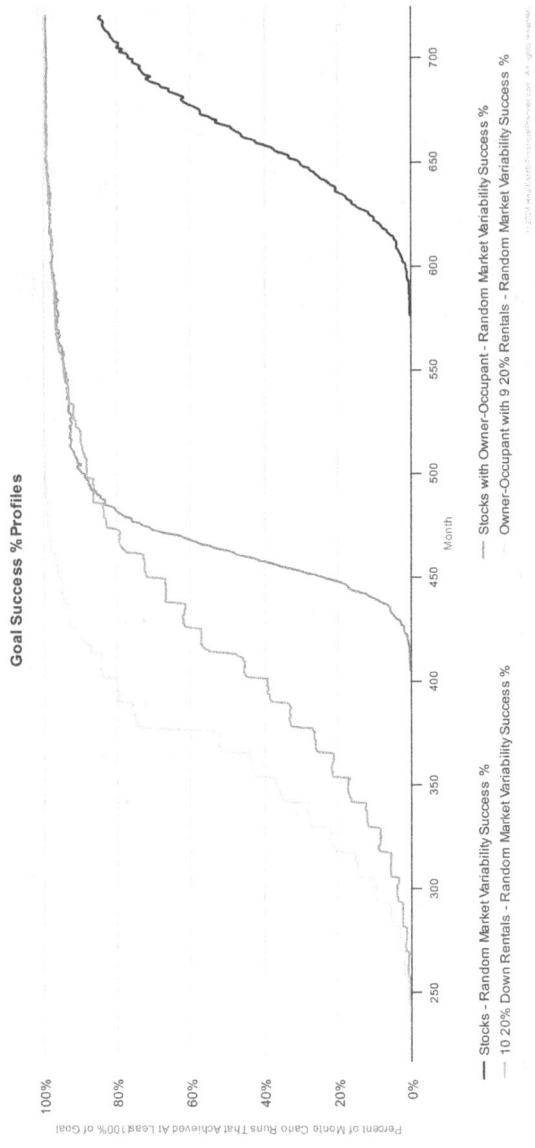

Goal Success % Profiles

Figure 22

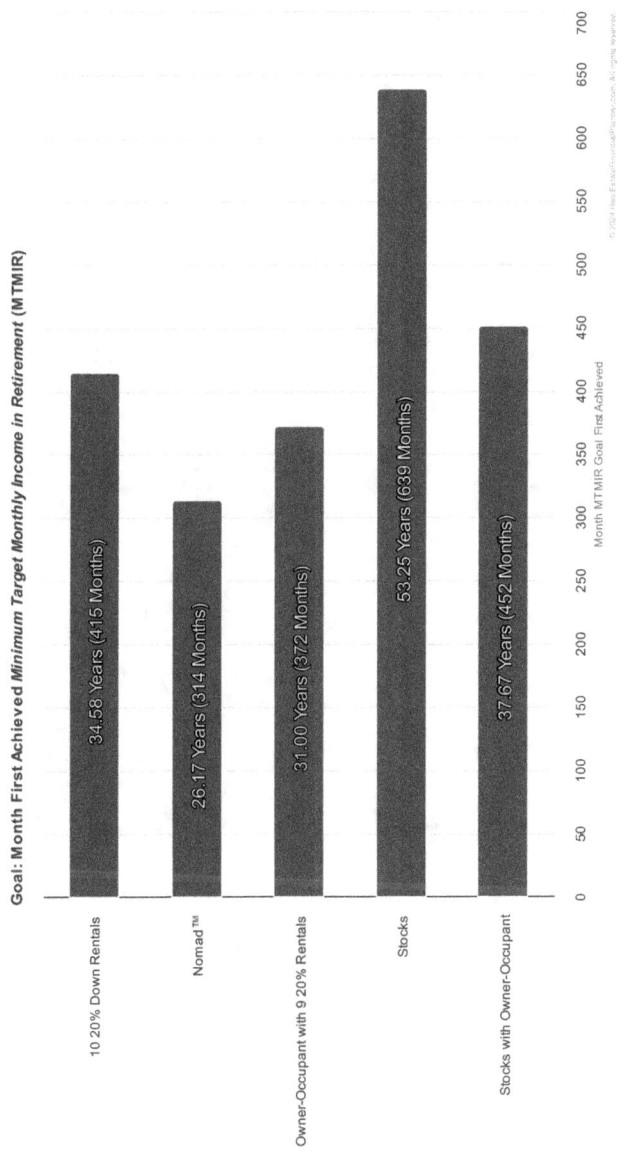

Goal: Month First Achieved *Minimum Target Monthly Income in Retirement* (MTMIR)

- 10 20% Down Rentals — 34.58 Years (415 Months)
- Nomad™ — 26.17 Years (314 Months)
- Owner-Occupant with 9 20% Rentals — 31.00 Years (372 Months)
- Stocks — 53.25 Years (639 Months)
- Stocks with Owner-Occupant — 37.67 Years (452 Months)

Month MTMIR Goal First Achieved

Figure 23

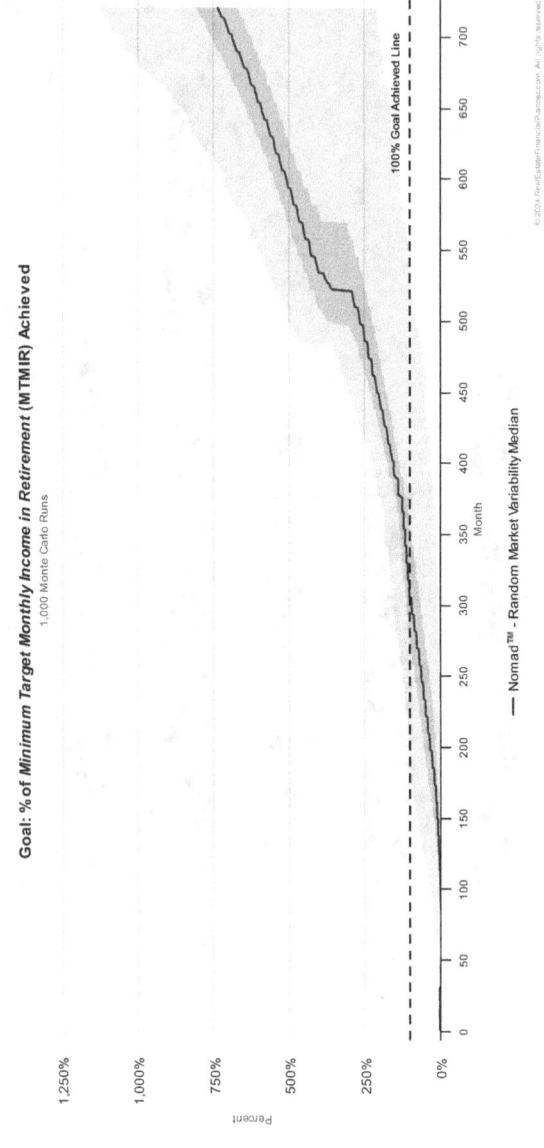

Goal: % of Minimum Target Monthly Income in Retirement (MTMIR) Achieved

1,000 Monte Carlo Runs

100% Goal Achieved Line

— Nomad™ - Random Market Variability Median

Figure 24

Figure 25

Figure 26

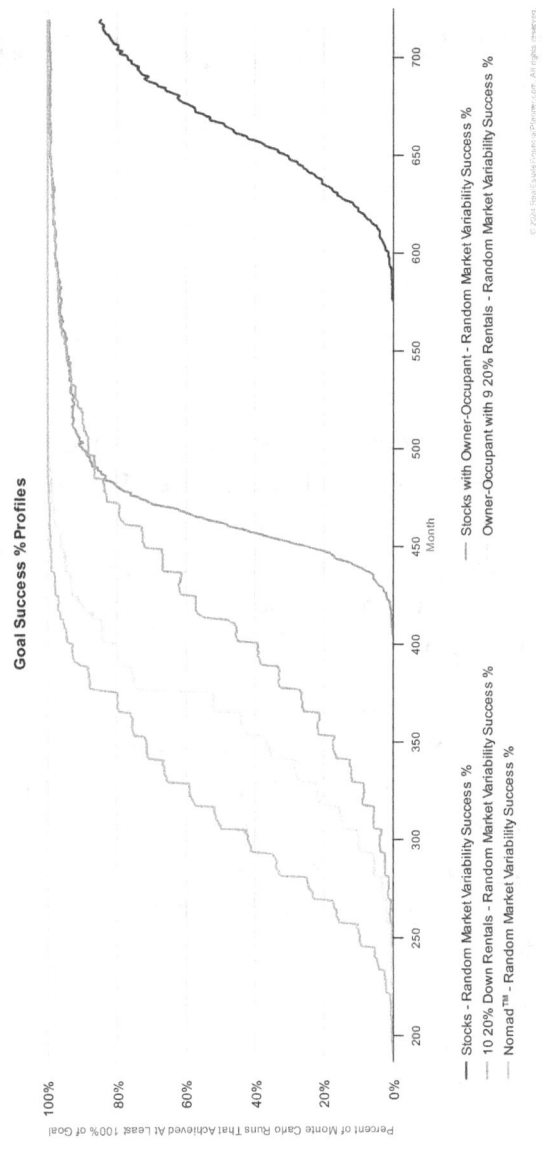

Figure 27

About the Author

James Orr is a seasoned real estate investor and the visionary creator of the Real Estate Financial Planner™ software. With a passion for sharing his wealth of knowledge, James has authored numerous books on real estate investing, covering a wide array of topics to help both novice and experienced investors succeed.

Living in Loveland, Colorado, James enjoys a fulfilling life with his wife, Tammy, whom he has been happily married to since 1995. Together, they have raised two grown sons. When he's not writing or managing his real estate investments, James is dedicated to teaching others the secrets of financial independence through smart property investments.

Also by James Orr

- The Real Estate Investing Mentor series of topic books
- How to Achieve Financial Independence and Live Your Passion Regardless of Age or Income: 10 Paths to Financial Independence Analyzed
- How to Acquire a Multi-Million Dollar Real Estate Portfolio With Just $3,000
- How to Acquire a Multi-Million Dollar Real Estate Portfolio Earning Just $5,000 Per Month
- Nomad™
- Ultimate Nomad™ Checklist
- Northern Colorado Real Estate Advisor
- Acquiring a Portfolio of Cash Flowing Properties In Northern Colorado: A Real Estate Financial Planner™ Blueprint
- Real Estate Investing Systems

Software and Spreadsheets

- Real Estate Financial Planner™ software
- The World's Greatest Real Estate Deal Analysis Spreadsheet™
- Should I Sell My Rental Property Spreadsheet™
- Should I Refinance My Rental Property Spreadsheet™
- CapEx Estimator for Rental Property – Basic and Advanced Spreadsheets
- Financial Independence Asset Allocation and Cash Flow Engines Spreadsheet™
- The Investor's Agent One-Page Business Plan™

A Small Request

Thank you for reading *The Real Estate Investing Mentor: The Affordable $50K Coaching Alternative* topic book on **Introduction to Nomad™ Real Estate Investing.**

I am positive if you follow what I've written, you will be on your way to successfully investing in real estate. When you do please reach out and share your story.

I have a small, quick favor to ask. Would you mind taking a minute or two and leaving an honest review for this book on Amazon?

Reviews are the BEST way to help others purchase this book and keep the price of my books low for everyone, and I check all my reviews looking for helpful feedback.

Please visit:

https://REFP.info/intro-nomad-book

Questions?

Thank you for taking the time to read this book. If a concept sparked a question or if you feel there's an area that could be explained more clearly, I'd truly appreciate hearing from you. You can reach me at **jamesorr@gmail.com** with any feedback specific to this title. My goal is to make each book as helpful and practical as possible, and your input plays a big part in that.

Just a note—while I'm here to help deepen your understanding of this book's topics, this isn't intended as a personal coaching service. For advice tailored to your own situation, I encourage you to work closely with a real estate agent who can provide the insight and support unique to your goals.

Thank you again for reading, and for helping me make this series an even better resource for investors like you.

www.ingramcontent.com/pod-product-compliance
Lightning Source LLC
Chambersburg PA
CBHW071508220526
45472CB00003B/955